ACCELERATED SANCTIFICATION
AND HEALING THE BROKEN HEARTED

The Spirit of the Sovereign Lord is on me, because the Lord has anointed me (us) to proclaim good news to the poor. He has sent me to bind up the broken hearted, to proclaim freedom for the captives and release from darkness for the prisoners.....

Isaiah 61:1 (NIV)

DAN & SUE CHICK

Revised April 2006

1st Edition	2004
2nd Edition	2006
3rd Edition	2010
4th Edition	2014
5th Edition	2015

Accelerated Sanctification
and Healing the Broken Hearted
by Dan & Sue Chick

Printed in the United States of America.

ISBN 9781498438155

For information on how to obtain copies of this workbook, please go to the following email: dan.d.chick@gmail.com. You may contact Dan and Sue Chick at (613) 832-8211.

www.xulonpress.com

TABLE OF CONTENTS

ACKNOWLEDGEMENT

*T*he material in this book is the culmination of thirty-six years of training on our part. Our knowledge base of the concepts of inner healing continues to evolve on an almost daily basis.

In the fall of 2003, Sue and I taught a twelve part series to our congregation on Sunday mornings. We would like to thank all the members of our core Leadership Team for having the heart to want to pursue God in learning how to accelerate the people's sanctification and the desire to put these concepts into practice within the body of Christ. We wish to thank Tom Moorhead and the rest of the Leadership who repeatedly encouraged us to deliver this teaching series.

We would like to acknowledge the blessing that our Leadership Team is to us for always allowing us to flow in the river of God. They have shown us much grace and mercy since the very genesis of our little vibrant church in December of 1996.

With heartfelt thanks, Sue and I would like to publicly thank Guy Robitaille for the hours, days, and many, very late nights he spent to make this workbook and training manual a reality. Sue and I have known Guy for over twenty-nine years; initially as his Pastors shortly after he first gave his life to the Lord. A close relationship was developed and continues to exist today.

As he began to grasp the concepts of inner healing that Sue and I taught, it had been his idea and desire to one day help me write a book on Christian Accelerated Sanctification and inner healing. His journalistic background and skills have been invaluable, as I have watched him pen our knowledge and teachings of the subject matter. Sue and I provided the content and from there, Guy rewrote, organized, and formatted all of that content in an effort to make this workbook something that is simple enough for old and new believers alike; to use for themselves and others.

We so appreciate Karen Tapp, who worked to shorten this book by taking out extra space and making it look more professional. A big thank you to Robyn Adams who spent months editing it and helping us so it was ready to send. We were overwhelmed when Ginette Pharand offered to translate the whole book into French, Hallelujah! We also thank Xulon Press for helping us publish it and get it out to the world. We feel it is worth two years of bible school in showing us how to become sanctified and useful in the Kingdom of God.

We would also like to thank our children for enduring the many hours spent in counseling sessions, with literally thousands of individuals over the past twenty-six years, since being introduced to the concept of inner healing. They have sacrificed much for their parents. So, Darren Chick, Holly Morris, and Amy Jones, Mom and Dad love you and thank you for the grace, mercy, and patience you have shown to us over the years of our ministry.

Dan & Sue Chick (613)832-8211
Canada
December 2006
dan.d.chick@gmail.com

FOREWORD

Reverends Dan & Sue Chick were born in the United States. They were in Kenya and Uganda in 1986 as missionaries for 2 ½ years. In 1989 they felt God's calling on their lives to be missionaries to Canada. They have raised up and turned River of Life Christian Fellowship over to Sandra Stott, and the leadership in Arnprior in 2012, Ontario, Canada.

From the very beginning of their ministry days some thirty-seven years ago, Dan and Sue have had a heart for **healing the broken-hearted and setting the captives free.** Their experience and knowledge of the subject matter is paramount. The wisdom that God has blessed Dan and Sue with regarding this subject is far reaching; well beyond what you will find in this workbook. Their understanding on the subject of sanctification and inner healing has evolved over the years, to where you will find their latest views in this workbook. It is only through Jesus Christ and the power of the Holy Spirit, that they allow themselves to be used as vessels to convey this knowledge.

Dan and Sue gained further knowledge of the subject area, modeled on Jesus as our Cornerstone, from Dr. Morris Smith, while attending Bible College at Elim Fellowship in 1980. They have studied many other resources and books and have attended seminars by Rev. Bill Gothard; Rev. John and Paula Sandford; Dr. Grant Mullen; Rev. Gerald and Marie Richards, and Rev. Chester and Betsy Kylstra. They have also spent considerable time studying books written by these same authors. It should also be noted that a significant portion of the material in this book has come directly from the book titled *Restoring the Foundation,* by Chester and Betsy Kylstra. The Chicks feel this book best reflects their heart in this area. Therefore quotes from the Kylstra's book, and other books are footnoted throughout this workbook. The descriptions of the footnotes are annotated at the back of the workbook in the bibliography.

Despite all the resources currently available, the whole subject of inner healing or Accelerated Sanctification still seemed mystical and complex. This was in essence the genesis of this workbook and training manual. The Kylstra's book, along with most of the others written by the seminar speakers mentioned above, were written to assist Pastors and Counselors in the area of inner healing. This workbook is designed for lay-Christians who are just getting started. This tool therefore, is an attempt to take the best of many other resources and create a simple method to deal with spiritual baggage in the lives of believers. This workbook also attempts to de-mystify the subject of 'getting rid of the past' so we can become who God made us to be.

Many of the other books related to this subject available to us are designed to show much more thoroughly and deeply the <u>concepts</u> of Christian renewal and living. What differentiates this workbook from others is an attempt on our part to develop a <u>process</u>. That if followed, will have a huge impact in the lives of new believers or older Christians who have not dealt appropriately with the issues from their past. Sanctification is the way of cleansing our life from anything that prevents us from being free to be used by the Master any day of our life. It is our goal that once you have experienced some degree of freedom in your individual lives, you too, will then be equipped to walk others through this process. Jesus didn't instruct us to *make converts*, rather to *make disciples*. This healing is simply part of the process of discipling one another.

This model is described in scripture in **Ex. 18:17-27**. In this passage, Moses was becoming overwhelmed with the amount of responsibility on his shoulders to settle disputes, so he appointed capable men (and women) to take up the slack so to speak.

It is this same principle we desire to foster at River of Life Christian Fellowship. We desire every member to realize they can minister in Jesus Christ. This means that walking through the process of Accelerated Sanctification with individuals should not only be reserved for our Pastors and leaders, but also for each of you who are taking the time to read this book. By applying the principles in this workbook, in your own personal lives, and by virtue of your commitment to Jesus Christ, our Lord and Savior; you too can share in the process of setting the captives free, and discipling them, so they can be useful in the Saviors hands.

Now, we urge you to begin *your* journey with us, as we take you step by step through an *"inner healing"* experience that you won't soon forget. After all, sanctification is the ABC's of the Kingdom, making a list of people who have hurt us, forgiveness, repentance and prayer.

It works! Just ask anyone who has been set free as a result of following the principles contained in this workbook. Some pastors use the book as a home group teaching.

Guy Robitaille
River of Life Christian Fellowship

Chapter 1

BACKGROUND

Why We Need Accelerated Sanctification (Inner Healing)

In this section, we will be outlining why inner healing is necessary in the lives of Christians and pre-Christians. We will also be describing the three laws that will help us to accept and apply the inner healing concepts and forgiveness.

Definition: When we use the term *"Accelerated Sanctification"*, we are strictly referring to the redemptive work of Jesus Christ on the cross, as applied to the lives of believers through the power of the Holy Spirit.

I had a vision… One day I was asking God why Christians' emotions seemed to go up and down as they struggled to maintain a healthy relationship with Him. It seemed many struggled for many years and still found no peace and joy as Christians.

He showed me a vision of a one year old baby wearing a diaper with a large rope around his waist. Then I saw Jesus kneeling down with His hands outstretched saying, "Come on. Walk to me." The baby carefully stood up and started tottering toward Jesus. Suddenly, the rope was pulled and the baby fell down. I looked at the other end of the rope and there was the enemy. He had pulled the rope and prevented the baby's walk toward Jesus.

Then I heard God say, "I'm going to teach you how to cut off the rope." In this current day, God has brought revelation through many pioneers of the faith in the whole area of healing the past concept.—*Sue Chick*

The *first* reason accelerated sanctification is important in our walk is because Jesus first modeled this ministry on earth. Furthermore, before His resurrection, He taught us that we were to do the same things: Fortunately for us, the Holy Spirit was sent to guide us and help us carry out these principles that are all based on the word of God, our Holy Bible.

Jesus said in **Luke 4:18-19**

> **18** *The Spirit of the Lord is on me, because He has anointed me to proclaim good news to the poor. He has sent me to proclaim freedom for the prisoners and recovery of sight for the blind, to set the oppressed free, 19 to proclaim the year of the Lord's favor."*

Then He said in **John 17:18** *"as you sent me into the world, I have sent them into the world."*

The *second* reason we need inner healing originates from a basic misunderstanding of the scripture in **2 Cor. 5:17** that says *"old things have passed away; behold, all things have become new." (NKJV)*

Jesus has indeed removed our sins which were against us, as He describes in **Eph. 2:6** *"and seated us with him in the heavenly realms in Jesus Christ."* This is our position in Christ. We have been forgiven and given eternal life, but we still need to participate in the "work" of sanctification. This is done by bringing each hurt, wrong and judgment...to the cross for appropriate repentance, forgiveness, and prayer. These are the ABC's of following Christ. From this point on we will use the words of Accelerated Sanctification and Inner Healing interchangeably since this IS the way to get *Sanctified* and *Healed* and *Prepared* for the Master's use.

In the book of Esther, before she could see the king, she needed six months of cleansing treatments (getting rid of the old) and 6 months of special perfumes and ointments (getting the fragrance of Christ, His anointing by the Holy Spirit, and an understanding of who we are in Christ).

Cleansing	from the old self	old belief system
Perfumes	taking in the fragrance of Christ	new belief system
Ointments	anointing of the Holy Spirit	presence/power of the Holy Spirit

We would suggest for example, that you didn't forget who you were or where you lived when you received Christ as your Savior. You were still *you* along with all the hurts from your past; your disappointments, physical and emotional illnesses...

2 Cor. 7:1

> *Since we have these promises, dear friends, let us purify ourselves from everything that contaminates body and spirit, perfecting holiness out of reverence for God.* See also **2 Cor. 5:17**

One can only assume from this passage that many of the sick and oppressed He healed were individuals who were believers, not only unbelievers. Therefore, inner healing applies to believers because we still suffer physically and emotionally.

The *third* reason we need inner healing is that hurts, generational sin patterns, disappointments and life traumas have opened us up to lies, vows, ungodly beliefs and bondage in our unredeemed soul. These hinder us from attaining our full potential in Christ. This is what Sue and I feel is the primary factor why the body of Christ *"altogether,"* has not been able to ARISE and accomplish God's purposes on the earth.

The accumulation of past hurts, shameful acts, broken relationships, embarrassing circumstances, etc., can be as much a problem to us as having a full grown tiger in the basement of our house. We would always have to make sure the door is closed and would spend much energy and worry about what would happen if the tiger got out.

Likewise, in the absence of sanctification or inner healing in a believer's life, it takes significant emotional energy to hide all these hurts, as well as creating the inability to be transparent, for fear that we would be judged and those around us would stop loving us or think less of us. We might even fear that it would permanently damage our reputation. Have you ever left the garbage under the sink too long? How can you tell? When you enter the house, the whole house smells rotten, right? With that smell in the house, no food or meal would be appetizing. In the same way, not resolving our past hurts, shameful acts before or after receiving Jesus Christ, broken or failed relationships, embarrassing circumstances, etc., can make you continually feel bad about yourself, just as garbage left under the kitchen sink can make the whole house smell bad. Although the inner healing process involves work on our part to get it all resolved, it is well worth the effort in order to feel good about ourselves and fully understand and believe who we are in Christ.

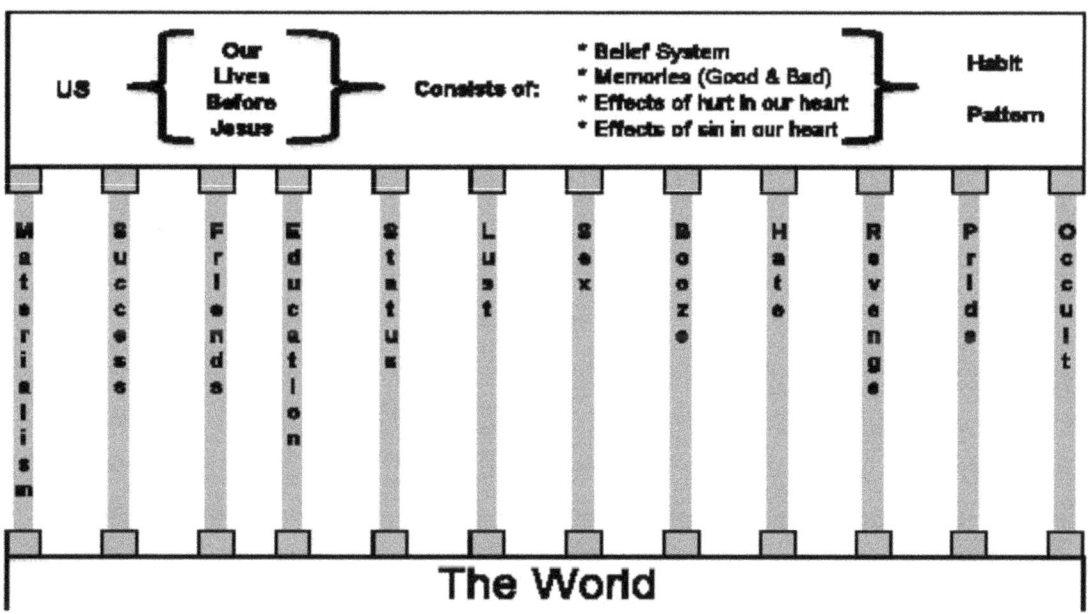

What we think after we receive Jesus Christ

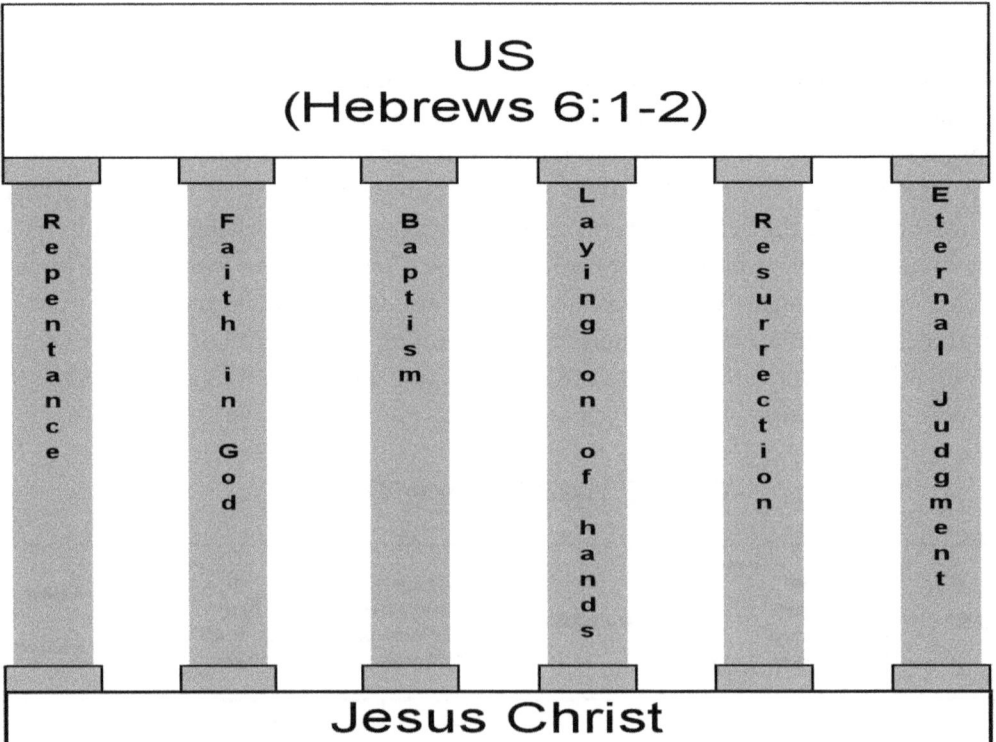

Reality

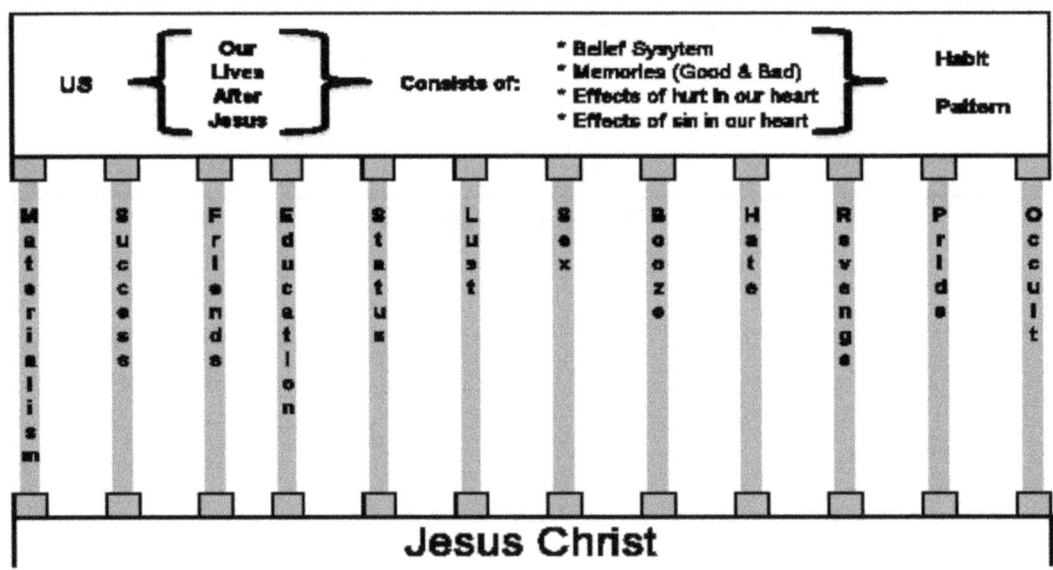

Three Spiritual Laws
- o **Law of Increase**
- o **Law of Sowing and Reaping**
- o **Law of Forgiveness**

The first law I want to cover is the *law of increase*. God initiated this law in the garden when He said:

Gen. 1:26-28

> *"Let us make man in Our image, according to Our likeness; let them have dominion over the fish of the sea, over the birds of the air, and over the cattle, over all the earth and over every creeping thing that creeps on the earth* **27** *So God created man in His own image; in the image of God He created him; male and female He created them.* **28 Then** *God blessed them, and said to them, "Be fruitful and multiply,"*

The law of increase concerning people in God's kingdom is the opposite of the world in which we live. The world is governed by laws that God made, like the second law of thermodynamics. It is a law that came about because of the fall of man; it did not exist before the fall, but is now true. The law of thermodynamics is a law of physics and should not be confused with one of the three spiritual laws being discussed in this section.

We believe that because man fell into sin for the first time (**Gen. 3:1-19**), God cursed the ground and this was the time when sickness, disease and weeds came to the earth and evil openly invaded the cosmos.

The second law of thermodynamics is a *tendency*. The second law states that it takes energy to cause wood to rot; oxygen and moisture before steel will rust; earthquakes and gravity cause houses to collapse or slide downhill. This law tells us what energy tends to do in the future; though I admit that in many cases the future can be only seconds, I think it is also possible for the future to be thousands of years. Aren't things everywhere falling apart by themselves? Doesn't wood rot, steel rust and buildings crumble? Everything is moving towards chaos. Entropy wins.

Entropy is the term in physics used as a measure of disorder. Physicists note that entropy in the cosmos is forever increasing; disorder, not order, is ever increasing. An example of this is when you fill your gas tank. It has zero entropy100 percent energy that can be used when you drive the car. As you drive the car, about 25 percent of the fuel is useable to help propel the car, and approximately 75 percent is wasted or unusable. Once you use the gas, you cannot get it back into your tank. You have to pay to get new gas. This is the curse that God put into the cosmos. Everything runs down.

For example, there were eight people when Noah went into the ark in about 2,300. Twenty-three hundred years later, when Jesus Christ was born, there were approximately one hundred million people on the earth. This illustrates the law of increase. On the other hand, when Noah went into the ark, there were none of the eight people in slavery. Yet 2,300 years later, at the time of the birth of Christ, about 95 percent of the population of the world was in slavery. This illustrates the second law of thermodynamics as applied to human nature. Our morals are decaying. Everything is going downhill.

The second law of thermodynamics applies to things involving matter and energy. However, this includes our physical body and our soul because we are matter and energy. All people die and everything growing dies also. It turns to dust, like the Bible says. Isn't that going toward chaos? The statement about the second law is like saying that the level of the water in a half-empty glass will change in only one way, go down toward completely empty...i.e. things won't stay as they are; they tend to deteriorate as predicted by the second law of thermodynamics. The second law demands that any spontaneous energy growth is directional. It has to spread out, only to go "downhill", never spontaneously in the opposite direction..."uphill".

The second law of thermodynamics applies only to matter and energy (which includes us), but God's law of increase applies to all we say or do and it will increase. Does the population of the earth grow yearly? Yes. Did you know the whole federal budget of the entire U.S. government in 1933 was three billion dollars, and that now it is the typical deficit for a city or province? If you plant a kernel of corn, do you expect it to produce one kernel in return or hundreds of kernels? This also illustrates the law of increase. Why did Jesus warn us that every word we say will be judged, because of the law of increase? When we realize that our actions and words: good or bad, will cause increase, it helps us to decide to perform only good actions and speak only good words.

Have you noticed how angry words spoken to someone does more damage than the words themselves would normally do? Words have the power to create images and thoughts, which is all part of being like God. Creativity turned in the wrong direction is negative not positive. Do you remember when someone said "I love you" to you? Yes, you do. These all illustrate the law of increase. Have you noticed what happens if you don't maintain relationships, like friendships or marriages? They deteriorate if they're not maintained, so unfortunately we must find out what increases automatically and what declines automatically. They say, "What goes around, comes around", usually with increase, unfortunately. From the second law we learn that all relationships with God or people will go downhill unless we maintain them and we can see that the words we speak will move toward disorder unless we keep resetting them to the positive.

God initiated the law in the garden when He said:

Gen. 1:26-28

> **26 Then God said,** "*Let us make man in Our image, according to Our likeness; let them have dominion over the fish of the sea, over the birds of the air, over the cattle, over all the earth and over every creeping thing that creeps on the earth.*" **27** *So God created man in His own image; in the image of God He created him; male and female He created them.* **28** *Then God blessed them, and said to them, "Be fruitful and multiply; fill the earth and subdue it, have dominion over the fish of the sea, over the birds of the air, and over every living creature that moves on the earth.*

The Law of Sowing and Reaping

The *law of sowing and reaping* says whatever we plant will grow up. If we plant corn, we will reap corn; if we plant peas, we will reap peas.

Gal. 6:7-10

> **7** *Do not be deceived: God cannot be mocked. A man reaps what he sows.* **8** *Whoever sows to please their flesh, from the flesh will reap destruction; whoever sows to please the Spirit, from*

the Spirit will reap eternal life. **9***Let us not become weary in doing good, for at the proper time we will reap a harvest if we do not give up.* **10***Therefore, as we have opportunity, let us do good to all people, especially to those who belong to the family of believers.*

If we plant anger, anger will come back, but, to our horror, it will usually come back with increase.

Example

I was once on a church board, and I noticed that no one listened to anything I said. This troubled me and eventually I asked God why. He pointed out that I was not listening to people, so they were not listening to me. I repented and started to listen. At the next board meeting, the pastor asked me for my opinion on an issue. What changed? What I sowed, I received...I started listening to them, and lo and behold: they started to listen to me.

Do you see how both the law of increase and the law of sowing and reaping work together? We sow something small, it increases and comes back larger. If we plant love and acceptance, we will receive love and acceptance. If we plant judgment of people, we will be judged; only we will be judged more harshly because of the law of increase. This works in our hearts and minds also. If we allow our minds to ruminate on judgmental thoughts, we will become preoccupied with negative thoughts and eventually this will lead to paranoia. It will also make your life miserable for there will be little, if any, joy in your life.

The same principle applies to tithing. If you find yourself in constant financial difficulty and crises, are you tithing? The law of sowing and reaping and the law of increase are at work in the area of *tithing* as well.

The Law of Forgiveness

I define *forgiveness* as "the elimination of all desire for revenge and personal ill-will toward those who deeply wrong or betray us." This elimination usually brings an *inner peace of heart* and the *freedom* of NOT having our lives defined by the injuries we have suffered.

Forgiving is especially for serious betrayals and wrongs. It is distinguished from *excusing*, which applies to less serious injuries or irritations. It is also distinguished from *pardoning*, which simply releases the victim from punishment. Forgiving is not the same as *accepting* or *understanding*. Forgiving is reserved for acts, which, in the view of the one injured, are *not* acceptable and *not* justifiable.

In Psychological Literature Forgiveness is Further Described as:
- A powerful therapeutic intervention and as an intellectual exercise in which the patient makes a decision to forgive. (Fitzgibbons, 1986)
- A voluntary act and a decision about how one deals with the past. (Hope, 1986)
- A letting-go of a record of wrongs and a need for vengeance and releasing associated negative feelings such as bitterness and resentment. (DiBlasio, 1992)
- The accomplishment of mastery over a wound and the process, through which an injured person first fights off, then embraces, then conquers a situation that nearly destroyed him. (Flanigan, 1992)
- Giving up one's right to hurt back. (Pingleton, 1989)
- Both intrapsychic and interpersonal. (Benson, 1992)

Theologically, one cannot consider the forgiveness of another person outside the context of *God's* forgiveness.

Forgiveness is Not:
- **Excusing or condoning a wrong** because "everyone does it" or someone "couldn't help it." It never approves or justifies behavior that is evil, wrong or reprehensible.
- **Treating a wrong as if it didn't matter** or denying that you've been hurt. We can only forgive those we (rightfully) blame for hurting us.
- **"Forgetting it"**, as if we strike a delete key and our brains go blank. Forgetting is evil because we lose the bloody lessons that the history of hatred teaches.
- **Canceling the consequences** for destructive or illegal behavior. There must always be accountability for our actions. During Christmas 1983, Pope John Paul II visited Mehmet Ali Agca in jail. The Pope forgave the man who shot him, calling Agca "my brother". But this didn't remove the consequences–imprisonment–for Agca's heinous act. Nor did the Pope suggest it should.
- **Given because the offender deserves it** or has earned it by repenting. Christ forgave His executioners despite their lack of repentance or their deservedness. Forgiveness depends not on the offender's behavior, but on the desire of the person who was wronged to heal and be healed. **(Rom. 5:6-11)**
- **Reconciliation or restoration** to one's former position of trust or power. A wife who forgives her husband for abuse shouldn't automatically be expected to return to him. Returning to her husband may not be wise or safe, depending on the circumstances.
  Reconciliation requires repentance and a real change of heart before a truly human, loving relationship is possible. *Reconciliation is the flower of which forgiveness is the seed.*
- **Something we do to obtain God's forgiveness**–a common misunderstanding of the Lord's Prayer: "forgive our sins, for we also forgive..." **(Luke 11:4)** For Jesus, forgiveness was a mark of *God's* gracious kingdom as described in **Matt. 18:21-35** and **Mark 2:1-12**. Refusing to forgive is actually a refusal of the kingdom and its forgiving *love*, which frees one from resentment. Refusing to forgive is, therefore, a *sin*.
  Forgiveness is all about US and very little about the offender

Forgiveness is one of the most *selfish* decisions we will ever make because it is mostly for our own good. It's not just a matter of principle or about the offender. Forgiveness is about ripping up the IOU and the desire to pay back or get even with someone who has hurt you. *Forgiveness is the only way to get beyond allowing the past from dominating our lives.* Unforgiveness causes us to focus on wrongs, hurts and anger and this results in our inability to live in the present. *Without forgiveness there is no present.*

Life is 10 percent about the circumstances from our past and 90 percent about how we process those circumstances, including what we experience on a daily basis in the present.

We either become victims, having no hope and no life, or we choose to forgive. *Forgiveness is an act of our will* and no more complicated than simply saying, "*Yes*, I choose to forgive so that I can be set free." Do you see why it's selfish? Most people on earth are focused on wrongs that have been done to them and thus have no joy, hope, or love flowing through them from God. Most of the circumstances from our past, which we focus on, become resentments and bitterness, and are, more often than not, exaggerated and false. "If we want mercy when *we* do wrong but want justice when others do wrong–this is contrary to the law of forgiveness. We need to choose mercy in both instances. It can't be one sided."(1)

It has been said that it is False Evidence Appearing Real (Fear) that keeps most of us in bondage to the past. Fear is also Faith in Evil. Not only are we in bondage, but the person who inflicted the wrong is also held in spiritual bondage as a result of your unforgiveness. When we forgive, we release ourselves FIRST and them second, so they can change. The Bible can be summed up in one key word...*love*. Unforgiveness is the opposite of love and therefore is considered a *sin* in God's eyes.

(1) Forgiveness–John & Carol Arnott

There Are Four Types of People Who Have Hurt Us:
- There are those who are physically dead.
- There are those who don't know they hurt us.
- Those who know they have hurt us, but do not care.
- Those who know about it, but don't know what to do.

Our decision to forgive them is *not* primarily for their own good, because in most cases, our decision to forgive them won't affect them as much as us. It is a *selfish act* on our part; to desire a release from the circumstances of the past and the controlling affect it has on us today. This is what true forgiveness will do.

The Bible says forgive and you will be forgiven. It is not the method you choose to forgive that matters to God, but not doing it *will eventually cost you* your eternal life.

Heb. 12:15

> *See to it that no one falls short of the grace of God and that no bitter root grows up to cause trouble and defile many.*

Eph. 4:31-32

> **31** *Get rid of all bitterness, rage and anger, brawling and slander, along with every form of malice.* **32** *Be kind and compassionate to one another, forgiving each other, just as in Christ God forgave you.*

The Scriptures that helped us the most to forgive are:

Matt. 6:14-15

> **14** *For if you forgive other people when they sin against you, your heavenly Father will also forgive you.* **15** *But if you do not forgive others their sins, your Father will not forgive your sins.*

Matt. 18:21-22

> **21***Then Peter came to Jesus and asked, "Lord, how many times shall I forgive my brother or sister who sins against me? Up to seven times?"* **22***Jesus answered, "I tell you, not seven times, but seventy-seven times."*

Matt. 18:32-35

> **32***Then the master called the servant in. 'You wicked servant', he said, 'I canceled all that debt of yours because you begged me to.* **33***Shouldn't you have had mercy on your fellow servant just as I had on you?'* **34***In anger his master turned him over to the jailers to be tortured, until he should pay back all he owed.* **35***This is how my heavenly Father will treat each of you unless you forgive your brother or sister from your heart.*

2 Cor. 2:10-11

> **10***Anyone you forgive, I also forgive. And what I have forgiven, if there was anything to forgive, I have forgiven in the sight of Christ for your sake,* **11***in order that Satan might not outwit us. For we are not unaware of his schemes.*

Let's look at the life of Rev. Bernard Mutombo as an example. Bernard was a National Elder in Uganda. A group of individuals wanted to take over his church building and he refused to allow them to have it. For his diligence, he was falsely imprisoned for three months; then they broke one of his arms; he was put in jail a second time; they broke one of his legs and put him in jail again for three more months. They then broke a second arm and he was put in jail a fourth time for yet another three months. Would we be able to forgive the people who would do such a thing to us? Bernard completely forgave them. He understood the principle of forgiveness.

If we forgive those who have wronged us, we will mature and grow in grace for others and ourselves. Not only can forgiveness help us, it can also help the offender by releasing them from the bondage our unforgiveness causes. *They will find it difficult to change if we do not forgive.* (**Matt. 16-19**)

Conclusion

We hope you see the need for healing your broken hearts and being delivered from oppression. We hope you now can understand how the laws of increase, sowing and reaping and forgiveness work *for us* if we truly forgive others who have offended us and who continue to offend us. Choosing *not* to forgive, will create a chasm between you and God and you will never be able to fully experience all that God has for you.

Forgiveness truly is one of the few instances where selfishness is OKAY in our Christian walk. The law of increase means that our peace and fruit of the Spirit, as described in the Bible as promised to us, will increase if we sow peace and forgiveness.

The following sections of this workbook will take us through the step-by-step process of experiencing inner healing. It is a practical guide and requires a commitment on your part to seek God and to play an active role in your spiritual recovery. Humility, openness, transparency and courage will be required.

We recommend that a close, mature, non-judgmental, friend or prayer partner lead in this because, notes must be written of hurts and traumas to help find the LIES and the truths which need to be repeated for thirty days. The papers should be destroyed at end of the book.

However, "all things are possible with God." **Mark 10:27** He wants you to be set free so if you will seek Him with all of your heart, He will be found by you. With His help, there will be hope and tremendous fruit at the end of the process. To illustrate inner healing, think of a series of boulders on the road.

These boulders are impeding the process of receiving all that God promises for us in the Bible. On the other side of the boulders there is light; there is peace; there is joy; there is hope; there is strength; there is confidence, etc. You will have to climb over some of these boulders and for some you'll be able to walk around them.

As you persevere and are diligent with the process, you will begin to look back at these boulders that were once blocking your view of God's riches in glory for your life. They will become small pebbles to you, signifying your being set free from a hurt or a circumstance

Prayer

Lord, give us courage to follow through with this process. Help us to see the glimmer of hope on the other side of the boulders. Give us a vision now of the joy, peace and freedom that is ours for the taking. In Jesus' Name, we pray.

Chapter 2

GENERATIONAL SIN & RESULTING CURSES

What Are Generational Sins and How They Affect Us Today

Definition

*S*ins of the fathers represent the accumulation of *all* sins committed by our ancestors. It is the heart tendency that we inherit from our forefathers to rebel. *It is the propensity to sin*, particularly in ways that represent perversion and twisted character. The accumulation (increase) continues until God's conditions for repentance are met.

The Biblical Basis of Generational Sins and Curses Affecting Us Are:

Ex. 20:5

> *You shall not bow down to them or worship them; for I, the LORD your God, am a jealous God, punishing the children for the sins of the fathers to the third and fourth generation of those who hate me...*

Ex. 34:6-7

> *6And he passed in front of Moses, proclaiming, "The LORD, the LORD, the compassionate and gracious God, slow to anger, abounding in love and faithfulness, 7maintaining love to thousands, and forgiving wickedness, rebellion and sin. Yet He does not leave the guilty unpunished; he punishes the children and their children for the sin of the fathers to the third and fourth generation."*

Theories on How Generational Sins and Curses are Passed Down to US
- o   Genes
- o   Growing up environmental modeling

- o Natural consequence–law of sowing and reaping
- o Demonic opportunity

Lev. 26:40-42

> **40***But if they will confess their sins and the sins of their fathers–their treachery against me and their hostility toward me,* **41***which made me hostile toward them so that I sent them into the land of their enemies–then when their uncircumcised hearts are humbled and they pay for their sin,* **42***I will remember my covenant with Jacob and my covenant with Isaac and my covenant with Abraham.*

Neh. 9:2

> *Those of Israelite descent had separated themselves from all foreigners. They stood in their places and confessed their sins and the wickedness of their fathers.*

Now that we have seen how sins pass onto the next generation, let us review what the Bible says about *generational sins* and resulting *curses*.

Why are Generational Sins Passed Down?

- o God sees us as families, not like Westerners who are very individualistic. How often is "I'm the God of Abraham, Isaac and Jacob" mentioned in the bible?
- o God is not only merciful, but He is also just.
- o God requires confession and repentance for sin. Just as salvation is free, we must confess and repent. These are action words; we must do it ourselves. Just as inner healing requires action on our part, so does confession and repentance. It is not handed to us on a silver platter when we are saved. The condition of confession and repentance is mostly done because of sin such as idolatry, iniquity and lawlessness, etc. As a result of this, each person is responsible for his/her own confession and repentance. No one can do it for us. There is no easier, softer way.

The following is the historical account (Bible) of generational sins passed down from Abraham, Isaac, and Jacob (with Rebekah's help).

First Generation Lying and Deceiving–Abram

Gen. 12:10-20

> **10***Now there was a famine in the land, and Abram went down to Egypt to live there for a while because the famine was severe.* **11***As he was about to enter Egypt, he said to his wife Sarai, "I know what a beautiful woman you are.* **12***When the Egyptians see you, they will say, 'This is his wife'. Then they will kill me but will let you live.* **13***Say you are my sister, so that I will be treated well for your sake and my life will be spared because of you."* **14***When Abram came to Egypt, the Egyptians saw that she was a very beautiful woman.* **15***And when Pharaoh's officials saw her, they praised her to Pharaoh, and she was taken into his*

palace. **16***He treated Abram well for her sake, and Abram acquired sheep and cattle, male and female donkeys, menservants and maidservants, and camels.* **17***But the LORD inflicted serious disease on Pharaoh and his household because of Abram's wife Sarai.* **18***So Pharaoh summoned Abram. "What have you done to me?" he said. "Why didn't you tell me she was your wife?"* **19***Why did you say 'She is my sister', so that I took her to be my wife? Now then, here is your wife. Take her and go!"* **20***Then Pharaoh gave orders about Abram to his men, and they sent him on his way, with his wife and everything he had.*

In **Gen. 20** We see that Abram lied a second time about his wife Sarai.

Second Generation–Lying Isaac

Gen 26:1-11

1*Now there was a famine in the land–besides the earlier famine of Abraham's time–and Isaac went to Abimelech, king of the Philistines in Gerar.* **2***The LORD appeared to Isaac and said, "Do not go down to Egypt; live in the land where I tell you to live.* **3***Stay in this land for a while, and I will be with you and will bless you. For to you and your descendants I will give all these lands and will confirm the oath I swore to your father Abraham.* **4***I will make your descendants as numerous as the stars in the sky and will give them all these lands, and through your offspring all nations of the earth will be blessed,* **5***because Abraham obeyed me and kept my requirements, my commands, my decrees and my laws."*
6*So Isaac stayed in Gerar.* **7***When the men of that place asked him about his wife, he said, "She is my sister," because he was afraid to say "She is my wife." He thought "The men of this place might kill me on account of Rebekah, because she is beautiful."* **8***When Isaac had been there a long time, Abimelech king of the Philistines looked down from a window and saw Isaac caressing his wife Rebekah.* **9***So Abimelech summoned Isaac and said, "She is really your wife! Why did you say "She is my sister?" Isaac answered him, "Because I thought I might lose my life on account of her."* **10***Then Abimelech said, "What is this you have done to us? One of the men might have slept with your wife, and you would have brought guilt upon us."* **11***So Abimelech gave orders to all the people: "Anyone who molests this man or his wife shall surely be put to death."*

Third Generation–Lying Jacob

Gen. 27:5-29

5*Now Rebekah was listening as Isaac spoke to his son Esau. When Esau left for the open country to hunt game and bring it back,* **6***Rebekah said to her son Jacob, "Look, I overheard your father say to your brother Esau,* **7**"*Bring me some game and prepare me some tasty food to eat, so that I may give you my blessing in the presence of the LORD before I die."* **8***Now, my son, listen carefully and do what I tell you:* **9***go out to the flock and bring me two choice young goats, so I can prepare some tasty food for your father, just the way he likes it.* **10***Then* *take it to your father to eat, so that he may give you his blessing before he dies."* **1** *Jacob said to Rebekah his mother, "But my brother Esau is a hairy man, and I'm a man with smooth skin.* **12** *What if my father touches me? I would appear to be tricking him and would bring down a curse on myself rather than a blessing."* **13** *His mother said to him, "My son, let the curse fall on me. Just do what I say; go and get them for me."* **4** *So he went and got them and brought them to his mother, and she prepared some tasty food, just the way his father liked it.* **15** *Then Rebekah took the best clothes of Esau her older son, which she had in the house, and put them on her younger son Jacob.* **16** *She also covered his hands and the smooth part of his neck with the goatskins.* **17** *Then she handed to her son Jacob the tasty food and the bread she had made.* **18** *He went to his father and said, "My father." "Yes, my son", he answered. "Who is it?"*

19 *Jacob said to his father, "I am Esau, your firstborn. I have done as you told me. Please sit up and eat some of my game so that you may give me your blessing."* **20** *Isaac asked his son, "How did you find it so quickly, my son?" "The LORD your God gave me success", he replied.* **21** *Then Isaac said to Jacob, "Come near so I can touch you, my son, to know whether you really are my son Esau or not."* **22** *Jacob went close to his father Isaac, who touched him and said, "The voice is the voice of Jacob, but the hands are the hands of Esau."* **23** *He did not recognize him, for his hands were hairy like those of his brother Esau; so he blessed him.* **24** *"Are you really my son Esau?" he asked. "I am", he replied.* **25** *Then he said, "My son, bring me some of your game to eat, so that I may give you my blessing." Jacob brought it to him and he ate; and he brought some wine and he drank.* **26** *Then his father Isaac said to him, "Come here, my son and kiss me."* **27** *So he went to him and kissed him. When Isaac caught the smell of his clothes, he blessed him and said, "Ah, the smell of my son is like the smell of a field that the LORD has blessed.* **28** *May God give you of heaven's dew and of earth's richness an abundance of grain and new wine.* **29** *May nations serve you and peoples bow down to you. Be lord over your brothers, and may the sons of your mother bow down to you. May those who curse you be cursed and those who bless you be blessed."*

Resulting Curses from Generational Sins

Dan. 9:11

All Israel has transgressed your law and turned away, refusing to obey you. "Therefore the curses and sworn judgments written in the Law of Moses, the servant of God, have been poured out on us, because we have sinned against you.

Solution for the Problem of Generational Sins and Resulting Curses

1 John 1:8-10

8 *If we claim to be without sin, we deceive ourselves and the truth is not in us.* **9** *If we confess our sins, he is faithful and just and will forgive us our sins and purify us from all* *unrighteousness.* **10***If we claim we have not sinned, we make him out to be a liar and his word has no place in our lives.*

Gal. 3:13-14

13*Christ redeemed us from the curse of the law by becoming a curse for us, for it is written: "Cursed is everyone who is hung on a tree."* **4***He redeemed us in order that the blessing given to Abraham might come to the Gentiles through Christ Jesus, so that by faith we might receive the promise of the Spirit.*

John 20:23

If you forgive anyone his sins, they are forgiven; if you do not forgive them, they are not forgiven.

The Confession for the Sins of our Ancestors Must be done because:
o   Of our participation in the sins of our fathers.
o   Because of the tendency we may have inherited because of their sins.
o   Of our reaction to the sin.

Likewise, confession and repentance must be done on behalf of our ancestors and US. If we have neither copied the sin nor reacted to the sins of our ancestors, then confession and identificational repentance must be done for our children and us.

Forgiveness is not enough to stop generational sin and neither is repentance, although they are both necessary. The cross of Christ must be put between us and the sin to stop it. It must be appropriated for the sin just like salvation must be received personally. Money in the bank must be drawn out in order to use it. Likewise, the cross must be appropriated with confession and repentance for it to work!

Generational Sin Identification List [1]

This list is by no means all-inclusive or exhaustive. Begin by circling those here that apply to you or any ancestor you know of. Also ask the Lord to reveal any others.

Use the prayer list, and prayer points one through seven of the prayer directive for each grouping, individually. Then pray points eight and nine.

1. **Addictions**
    Alcohol; food; any prescription drugs/street drugs; hoarding; emotional and/or physical abuse; sexual sins; smoking; overworking; video games; television; internet; gambling; profanity; pornography; internet games

2. **Control**
    Possessiveness; manipulation; rebellion; unbelief; tardiness; uncleanness; criticalness; intimidation, co-dependency; stubbornness; domination; broken promises.

3. **Death**
    Disappointment; murder; miscarriages; untimely/traumatic death; abortion; stillbirth; unresolved grief/loss; war death; suicide

4. **Family/Culture**

   Hereditary diseases; broken marriage; divorce; unhealthy ties with biological and extended family; rebelliousness; father not teaching children the ways of God; abandonment; parental inversion; unworthiness; low self-esteem; unlawful actions; being an illegitimate child; family secrets; lack of communication; not feeling safe or loved

5. **Guilt and Fears**

   Death; destruction; hatred; bitterness; false guilt; shame; fears of all kinds

6. **Injustice**

   Being unfairly punished; favored siblings; blame spouse or self; lack of intimacy and communication; men dominant over women or opposite; sibling rivalry; fights; feuds; silent treatment

7. **Mental Illness**

   Anxiety; depression; bipolar disorder; ADD; ADHD; schizophrenia; phobias; oversleeping; withdrawal; isolation

8. **Money Extremes**

   Greed; poverty; status seeking; job robbery; curse of the devourer; overspending; stealing; business or financial losses; deceptive business practices

9. **Negative Emotions**

   Anger; bitterness; rage; violence; domination; fear; pride; resentment; hatred of men or women; emotional dependence; prejudice; revenge; jealousy; envy; lack of intimacy

10. **Physical Infirmities**

    Sickly; weak; unable to work; infirmities; sleep apnea; asthma; high blood pressure; heart disease; cancer; diabetes; disease of any kind

11. **Rejection**

    Divorce; separation; adoption; death; abuse; over-protection; isolation; perfectionism; rage; violence; insecurity; martyr/victim; self-pity; hopelessness; shame; betrayal; unfulfilled destinies

12. **Religious Restrictions/Oppression**

    Domination; control; other religions; cults (Mormons, Freemasonry, etc.); occult involvement (be specific); supernatural powers; psychic powers; idolatry; witchcraft; satanic ritual abuse

13. **Sexual Sins**

    Fornication; adultery; perversions; pornography; masturbation; abuse; rape; being illegitimate; molesting; incest; fantasizing

14. **Other**

    Pride; arrogance; lying

Note: Keep all of your completed lists in the workbook until you have walked through the entire process. You may need to refer back to them occasionally. It is also recommended that you keep a separate list (below) to document all the lies about yourself that will be uncovered as you go through the inner healing process. We will be covering ungodly beliefs in chapter 7, however, if you recognize any lies before you arrive at that chapter, write them down below

(1) Restoring the Foundations **page 125/***Family Patterns* **page 397 – by Rev. Chester and Betsey Kylstra**

Lies of UnGodly Beliefs

1.

2.

3.

4.

5.

6.

7.

Note:

It is much better to walk through this process with another individual then to do it alone.

As you pray the prayer below, fill in the blanks for each item on your list.

We suggest you pray one grouping at a time, by doing steps one through seven. Repeat this for all fourteen groupings. Then pray steps eight and nine for all groupings together. We recommend that you pray for every item in each of the groupings whether you have circled it or not, because none of us knows *everything* about our ancestors.

The purpose of circling the items in each grouping is to allow you to pray more fervently in those areas and to help you identify negative behavioral patterns in your own life which may be the result of the sins of your ancestors.

Prayer Generational Sins and Resulting Curses

1. I confess the sins or curses of _____. (Pray through one group at a time)
2. I choose to forgive and release _____ (names) for the sins, curses, and the Consequences I've found in my life (be specific) _____.
3. I ask you to forgive me, Lord, for these sins or curses; for yielding to them or reacting to them, and to the resulting curses. I receive your forgiveness.
4. On the basis of your forgiveness, Lord, I choose to forgive myself for any involvement in these sins or curses.
5. (Firmly declare) I renounce the sins and curses over the issues I've just mentioned and I BREAK this power from my life and the lives of my descendants, through the redemptive work of Christ on the cross.
6. (Firmly declare) I renounce and BREAK ANY agreement I have made with the devil over the issues I've just mentioned. I break ALL agreement with the power of darkness! I CANCEL all agreements made with demons, by myself or by any of my ancestors. I put the cross of Christ, between myself and any demonic activity due to ancestral sins or curses for all issues just mentioned.
7. I receive God's freedom from these sins and from the resulting curses. I receive _____ (the opposite of sins just mentioned).
8. Release me from the LIE that _____. (From each group) (Write down all lies. This is the best time to remember them)

9. We thank You Lord, that what we forbid on earth is forbidden in heaven and I forbid any demonic influence, now and forever in Jesus' Name!
    (After completing all areas)
10. LORD JESUS, fill me with the Holy Spirit, the love of God, my inheritance of hope in God and new faith in Jesus Christ!

1 General prayer ideas–*Restoring the Foundations* **page 153–Rev. Chester and Betsey Kylstra**

Chapter 3

SOUL/SPIRIT HURTS (HURTS TOWARD US)

Definition

A *soul/spirit hurt* is some type of emotional or spiritual wound that you received based on somebody else's words, actions, neglect, or rejection, which causes emotional, physical, or spiritual trauma.

Scriptures Relating to the Healing of Our Soul/Spirit Hurts

Isa 61:1-2
> **1** *The Spirit of the Sovereign LORD is on me, because the LORD has anointed me to preach good news to the poor. He has sent me to bind up the broken hearted, to proclaim freedom for the captives and release from darkness for the prisoners,* **2** *to proclaim the year of the LORD's favor and the day of vengeance of our God, to comfort all who mourn.*

Ps 147:3
> *He heals the brokenhearted and binds up their wounds.*

John 14:12
> *I tell you the truth, anyone who has faith in me will do what I have been doing. He will do even greater things than these, because I am going to the Father.*

The Biblical genesis of hurts and emotional wounds is from the fall of man in the Garden of Eden.

Gen 2:15-17
Gen 3:6-7
Gen 3:16-19
Gen 3:22-24

What Situations Cause Hurt? (1)

o   Death of a loved one
o   Divorce
o   Abortion
o   Abuse (physical, verbal, emotional, sexual)
o   War memories
o   Disability
o   Job loss
o   Accidents
o   Failures
o   Childlessness
o   Too many children

(1) Restoring the Foundations page209 Rev. Chester and Betsy Kylstra

Examples of Soul/Spirit Hurts

Sometimes hurts come from what was NOT done. I was once a manager and project engineer designing software with the General Electric Company. One day my superior calls me into his office and tells me that he wants me to work as a technician producing something he felt only I was capable of doing. The technician's position was four hierarchal levels below the position I had been occupying. Although he said he was sorry, and reiterated that he felt I was the only one capable of doing the job he was asking me to do, the result of this was a soul/spirit hurt. I did the job for 4 months but I resented it the whole time.

Another example of a soul/spirit hurt I experienced was as a child. Before my father went to war overseas, we had a great relationship. We would play together; go for walks together and just plain have fun together. Well then, he left to fight overseas and was gone for a full year. This alone resulted in soul/ spirit hurt as I could not fully comprehend why he was away for such a long period of time. This created a void in me. When he finally came back from the war a year later, he wasn't the same. The war had damaged his emotions so that he wasn't able to play and have fun with me like he did before he went to war.

Sometimes Hurts Come From What Was NOT Done! (2)

o   Toddler never hugged or cuddled
o   Child never made to feel special
o   Deep disappointments beyond our control
o   Children who failed to meet our expectations
o   Promotions that never come
o   Money problems
o   Ongoing arguments and distance from spouse

Consequences of Soul/Spirit Hurts (3)

o   Hurts begin in one person and affect the whole family
o   Hurts affect the entire person
o   Hurts cause others hurt–hurting people hurt people

31

- o   Hurts cause lies (ungodly beliefs) to be established
- o   Hurts cause ongoing vulnerability and hopelessness
- o   Hurts cause shame–feeling like we are made wrong and cannot be fixed
- o   Hurts cause defense mechanisms
- o   Hurts cause us to wear "masks"–pretend that we are something we are not
- o   Hurts cause restricted growth
- o   Hurts cause anger/disappointment with God
- o   Hurts cause blocked emotions
- o   Hurts cause fragmented personality
- o   Hurts lead to demonic oppression
- o   Hurts lead to sorrow/depression

(2)Restoring the Foundations–page 209 by Rev. Chester and Betsy Kylstra
(3)Restoring the Foundations–page 210 by Rev. Chester and Betsy Kylstra

Ps. 41:4
I said, "O LORD, have mercy on me; heal me, for I have sinned against you."

2 Cor. 7:1
Since we have these promises, dear friends, let us purify ourselves from everything that contaminates body and spirit, perfecting holiness out of reverence for God.

Forgiveness is a BIG part of healing soul/spirit hurts

Matt. 18:34-35
"34In anger his master turned him over to the jailers to be tortured until he should pay back all he owed. 35This is how my heavenly Father will treat each of you unless you forgive your brother from your heart." (This is one of the scariest verses in the Bible.)

<u>Some Hindrances That Block Receiving God's Healing of Soul/Spirit Hurts</u> (4)
- o   Not familiar with the process
- o   Unconfessed sin
- o   Unforgiveness
- o   Major fears
- o   Analytical thinking; administrative mind
- o   Medications
- o   Anger/disappointment with God
- o   Blocked emotions
- o   Demonic interference

(4) Restoring the Foundations–pages 217-227 Rev. Chester & Betsy Kylstra

How to Bring Healing From Hurts

A woman in her thirties felt like she was having a nervous breakdown. It suddenly occurred to her that she had been raped when she was thirteen years old. She had managed to suppress her thoughts and feelings surrounding the incident for all those years. She had been threatened by her abductor that if she told anyone, he would kill her and her family. She succumbed to this fear rather than risking injury to herself or her family.

She had always felt like she was a BAD girl; that somehow she had done something wrong. When we explained to her that all of the evil in this man was transmitted to her through the sexual union, she gasped saying, "You mean I'm not a bad person? I feel like a tremendous weight has been lifted from me." All of the shame began to melt from her as she dealt with the resulting problems of being raped. Today, you would not recognize her; her countenance has totally changed.

Make a List of Hurts

Either from present time back, or whenever God reveals. Start from the present and work your way back in time. Let the Holy Spirit guide you *Jesus wants us free*. Just sit alone with Him and ask Him to reveal all the deep hurts. He knows what they are because he was with you.

1 Cor. 13:57 tells us that God keeps no record of wrongs. *But we do*. A worksheet is provided for you below or use a separate piece of paper.

Soul/Spirit Hurts List (Hurts toward us)

Jesus wants us Free, just sit alone with God and listen. He wants you to be free more than you do! One line explanations is all that is required. The time he/she said or did..........

1.
2
3
4
5
6
7

Prayer for Soul/Spirit Hurts [5]

Concept: Take each individual hurt and pour out your complaint to the Lord!!
Psalm 142: 1-7, Psalm 142:2 (I pour out my complaint to Him; before Him I tell my trouble)
Be Real, **Be Transparent!! Don't Stuff it anymore!!** Freedom from the bondage of emotional pain is the goal here. Tell God how you feel! If feelings won't come; it may be necessary to command in Jesus' name that emotions be released.

Realize the need to forgive, not because they deserve it! Forgiveness is the most selfish thing we can do! If we want mercy, then it is required that we give mercy, let God keep the book on justice.

Matt. 18:33-35

> *Shouldn't you have had mercy on your fellow servant, just as I had mercy on you? In anger his master turned him over to be tortured, until he should pay back all that he owed* **35** *This is how our heavenly Father will treat each of you unless you forgive your brother from your heart.* (This is how important God thinks forgiveness is.)

PRAY

1. Lord Jesus, I pour out my complaint to you for this hurt _____. (Be sure to tell Jesus accurately how you felt at this time.)

2. I set my WILL to forgive and release _____ (names) from all punishment they are due. Forgive *me* Lord, for holding this hurt/sin against them.

3. I choose to forgive *myself* for the anger and resentment I have been harboring against them. Forgive *me* for all of *my* unforgiveness, Lord.

4. I release and give to You Father all my anger, hatred, grief, pain, sorrow, fear and shame _____ (and any other feelings).

5. (Firmly declare) I break all agreement with all *lies* the enemy placed in my life because of this hurt, especially the *lie* that _____ (be specific).

6. (Firmly declare) I renounce and break all agreements with this *lie* and the powers of darkness and I cancel all agreements with any demons, *now and forever*!
   (Leader should pray this for the one in process)

7. I *break* off the shock and trauma of this hurt, accident or situation! I break it off your mind and thought processes. I break it off your emotions or feelings. I break it off your will or decision making. I break it off your central nervous system. I break it off your body and all of your organs. I break it off your spirit in Jesus' name.

Note:

If you sense that this hurt is a very deep issue, ask them to go back into that moment and (*leader*) say: "Jesus, You were there at that very moment of time. Please come and reveal Yourself and *do* something to show your love. Come Jesus (wait for a moment or two, and then ask what's happening)." If they can't see Jesus, ask them if there is someone they need to forgive. (Unforgiveness blocks revelation). A parent, friend, enemy, themselves or God. It is <u>not</u> that God needs to be forgiven, but often we blame God for what He does or doesn't do.!! If nothing happens, go on to number eight.

8. I *choose to accept* and *believe* the TRUTH about this *soul/spirit hurt,* and that *God* never wanted this to happen to me and *only* wants good for my life.
   After all hurts are covered, pray this:

9. Lord, please *fill* me with Your Holy Spirit; washing all the areas of my life and replacing them with your healing and love!!

(5) Restoring the Foundations – general prayer idea–page 25

Chapter 4

BITTERROOT JUDGMENT AND BITTERROOT EXPECTANCY⁽²⁾

Definition of Bitterroot Judgment

Bitterroot Judgment is a form of unforgiveness. It is more than forming an accurate opinion about something someone else has said or done. It is holding them responsible for not measuring up to our specific code of conduct or action. Judgment is born out of anger and strife; and turns into a bitter root. Accurate appraisals are born out of love and a desire to see the other person turn away from some habit or character trait that is hampering their progress in life. When we judge someone, we hold that person in bondage, which in turn comes back on us (*law of sowing and reaping* and the *law of increase*). The more common forms of judgment are not honoring our parents; closing our hearts to our parents and becoming like the one we judge.

Rom. 14:13
> *Therefore let us stop passing judgment on one another. Instead, make up your mind not to put any stumbling block or obstacle in your brother's way.*

Heb. 12:15
> *See to it that no one falls short of the grace of God, and that no bitter root grows up to cause trouble and defile many.*

A good example of this would be someone who grows up in relative poverty and says to himself, "I will never live like this when I grow up." Another example could be if a child grows up in an alcoholic home and he says to himself that he will never become an alcoholic and do the things his parents did when they were drinking. This could be both a judgment and an inner vow.

Both of these result in judgments towards our parents because in order to feel this way, we are placing judgments against our parents and we lack respect towards them. What usually happens is we become alcoholics or live in poverty ourselves. We also might not drink, but be so bitter that we act bitter toward our family. Remember the law of increase? Do we want to become a worse alcoholic than our parents were? Do we want to live in relative poverty? Do we want to treat our family with bitterness?

(1) John and Paula Sandford videos–Elijah House

Judgments

Matt. 7:1-2

> **1***Do not judge, or you too will be judged.* **2***For in the same way you judge others, you will be judged, and with the measure you use, it will be measured to you.*

When we judge our parents, we activate three powerful laws of nature that work very strongly against us:

- o **The Law of Sowing and Reaping**
- o **The Law of Increase**
- o **The Law of Honoring Your Parents**

We have talked about the *law of sowing and reaping* and the *law of increase* in previous chapters. Let us now explore the *law of honoring our parents.*

The Law of Honoring Our Parents

Ex. 20:12

> *Honor your father and your mother, so that you may live long in the land the LORD your God is giving you.*

Matt. 15:4

> *For God said, "Honor your father and mother and anyone who curses his father or mother must be put to death."*

In our own strength, we cannot resist the results of these laws. Only the grace and mercy of God can overcome the effects of judging others. Let me remind you that no law of God is an inert, dead thing. The laws of God *will* operate whether we know of them or not; approve of them or disapprove; love them or hate them; believe or disbelieve. The law of God will be enacted.

Therefore, God's impartial laws originally meant to bless us will affect us whether we unintentionally activate them by judgments as children, or intentionally sin as adults. It makes no difference. Let me also suggest that in most cases, the judgment takes a lot of time before it returns to bite us. It often takes five to ten years to come into action. Therefore, our rational mind never connects the current difficulty with the judgments we made several years before.

The result of all this bitterroot judgment/expectancy and dishonoring our parents causes us to *close our hearts to our parents.*

Acts 28:27

> *For this people's heart has become calloused; they hardly hear with their ears, and they have closed their eyes. Otherwise they might see with their eyes, hear with their ears, understand with their hearts and turn, and I would heal them.*

Matt. 15:19

> *For out of the heart come evil thoughts, murder, adultery, sexual immorality, theft, false testimony, slander.*

Matt. 18:33-35

> **33***Shouldn't you have had mercy on your fellow servant just as I had on you?* **34***In anger his master turned him over to the jailers to be tortured, until he should pay back all he owed.* **35***This is how my heavenly Father will treat each of you unless you forgive your brother from your heart.*

If you sincerely pray the prayers at the end of this chapter, then we can ask God to do what He promises in:

Ezek. 36:25-27

> **25***I will sprinkle clean water on you, and you will be clean; I will cleanse you from all your impurities and from your idols.* **26***I will give you a new heart and put a new spirit in you; I will remove from you your heart of stone and give you a heart of flesh.* **27***And I will put my Spirit in you and move you to follow my decrees and be careful to keep my laws.*

This is our inheritance; a promise from God. We need only activate our faith to receive it.

BITTER ROOTS

We all understand that a tree has underground roots. These roots are the hidden support for the tree, giving it life and stability. In a person, these "roots" are habitual ways we receive nurture from God, from others, nature and ourselves. Our roots also lie below the surface, usually hidden from the adult mind. Adults usually rationalize away the majority of these roots. However, if we harbor bitter roots, we receive harm to ourselves.

Bitterroot Judgments[2]

Bitterroot judgments operate because of the unchangeable laws of God, which cause us to reap in kind what we have sown. In addition, the *laws of increase* make each repeated action multiply the "crop" we harvest for good or bad. Furthermore, bitterroot judgments have the power to contaminate not only ourselves but also those around us.

If we don't deal with our bitterroot attitudes, we become like a porcupine.

We allow people to get only so close, then we show them our *"prickly"* side. We appear as Jekyll and Hyde not only to those who observe us, but, more importantly, to those we are in a relationship with. We seem so nice in one instant but then we turn *"prickly"* at the drop of a hat and we push people away.

Let us begin dealing with our bitterness against others so we can live abundantly in peace and love while serving our Lord. This ought to be the desire of every believer.

Bitter Roots or Bitterroot Judgments are Several Things:
o   Our sinful reactions to hurt.
o   Condemning judgments we place on other people.
o   Refusal or inability to forgive someone.

Bitter roots are NOT the hurtful or terrible things that happened to us, nor are they the sins of those who have wronged us; *they are OUR sins.* They are NOT powerful enough to overcome the free will of another, though they do defile or taint our relationships with others. They can change our perspective of everything that people do in relation to us and by doing so, change our reactions to them. That is what happens in a physical sense, but in a spiritual sense we often refer to it as holding someone in spiritual bondage. What happens to *us* as a result is we are in the prison right next to them. This also causes a spirit of offense and a deception of *unbelief.* We don't realize this because we are blinded by *denial.*

(2) The Transformation of the Inner Man–John and Paula Sanford

Heb. 12:14-16
> **14***Make every effort to live in peace with all men and to be holy; without holiness no one will see the Lord.* **15***See to it that no one misses the grace of God and that no bitter root grows up to cause trouble and defile many.* **16***See that no one is sexually immoral, or is godless like Esau, who for a single meal sold his inheritance rights as the oldest son.*

Afterward, as you know, when he wanted to inherit this blessing, he was rejected. He could bring about no change of mind, though he sought the blessing with tears.

James 3:14-16
> **14***But if you harbor bitter envy and selfish ambition in your hearts, do not boast about it or deny the truth.* **15***Such "wisdom" does not come down from heaven but is earthly, unspiritual, of the devil.* **16***For where you have envy and selfish ambition, there you find disorder and every evil practice.*

Bitterroot Expectancy

What is Bitterroot Expectancy and how is it different from Bitterroot Judgment?

Mal. 4:5

He will turn the hearts of the fathers to their children, and the hearts of the children to their fathers; or else I will come and strike the land with a curse.

Expectancy is a psychological practice of our nature. Some people suggest that we draw to ourselves what we expect. Christians call them self-fulfilling prophecy. We *push* people to fulfill our picture of the way things will go.

Bitterroot Judgment vs. Bitterroot Expectancy

Bitterroot Judgment is everything concerning the past involving people and situations in which we made a judgment against. Without realizing it we live our life and make decisions according to them.

Bitterroot Expectancy is the result of a judgment, which causes us to *expect* in our present or future circumstances similar bad or negative things to happen.

An example of this in my own life is when I judged my father for leaving me when I was two years old, to serve in World War II. I expected things to go wrong in any significant relationship after that, including my relationship with my heavenly Father.

Examples

A young boy develops a *bitter expectancy* that he will always be criticized by his mother and thus in his early childhood he makes a powerful, condemning judgment against his mother. He soon forgets the judgment, but it has been sown as a seed (with the power to contaminate/defile), which will affect him. Chances are he will reap through his wife and other women what he experienced with his mother. Because of the forgotten nature of the sowing, the reaping may come as a surprise to him.

Another example is a child who grew up in a home where the mother was suicidal; had many sicknesses and thus spent much time in hospitals. The child might say to himself that he will never get sick so he becomes a health addict. He may also tell himself that he will never marry a woman who is prone to sicknesses, therefore exercising his own free will against that of God.

If he does marry a woman who is prone to sickness, he is very likely to be bitter about his situation and unable to exercise the necessary compassion and love his wife requires. This could also result in bitterness and a very unhealthy marriage.

Fruits of Bitterroot Judgment and Expectancy [3]
- o Anger
- o Accusation
- o Blaming
- o Complaining

- o Criticalness
- o Emotional turmoil
- o Fault finding
- o Frequent medical problems
- o Gossip
- o Inability to build lasting relationships (too judgmental)
- o Inability to love and express love
- o Inability to trust
- o Judging
- o Murmuring
- o Ridicule
- o Unforgiveness

These are but a few of the fruits of bitterroot judgment and expectancy.

Who is accountable? WE ARE!! God holds us accountable for our own sinful reactions to what happens to us. We are guilty but not condemned if we bring our sins to the *cross* to find healing.

How Do We Deal With These Bitter Roots? Through recognition, repentance and prayer!

Recognition–seeing the patterns and discussing how they affect our lives and those around us.

Repentance–choosing to change. Determining to stop patterns by bringing all those judgment and expectations to the cross in prayer.

Prayer – specific, focused, Spirit-led prayer will work miracles!

2 Cor. 10:5
> *We demolish arguments and every pretension that sets itself up against the knowledge of God, and we take captive every thought to make it obedient to Christ.*

Becoming Like the One We Judge or Hate
Many of us who are hurt by our parents as children, say in our hearts, that we will never be like them.
(3) John and Paula Sandford–Videos and Seminars

As we grow up, we focus on doing things right, not the way our parents did it, especially in raising our own children. However, usually over a period of ten to fifteen years, we become *just like them* to the point where our spouses say we are just like our dad or mom. Then we are very upset until we realize it is true and then we are horrified at its truth.

Why is this?

It is called *emotional focus*. Inside our subconscious, we keep thinking about what they did wrong. This is why it is called an *emotional focus*. Since we keep thinking about it, we become that way.

Scripture says in:

Rom. 2:1

You, therefore, have no excuse, you who passed judgment on someone else, for at whatever point you judge the other, you are condemning yourself, because you who pass judgment do the same things.

Prov. 23:7

For as he thinks within himself, so he is. (NASU)

How Do We Reverse All This?

How do we stop the effects of *bitterroot judgment and expectancy*; dishonoring our parents; closing our hearts to our parents or from becoming like them in a bad way?

First, we must recognize and expose the judgments we have made against our parents or others. I would recommend that you ask yourself this question: *What* did my parents do that bothered me as a child? Below, we have listed some of the things they might have done. Circle the ones that apply. It is incomplete, so therefore you need to go before God to ask Him to help you find where you judged or closed your heart to your parents. Start with the ones below and add the others God has or is revealing to you.

Judgment Identification List [4]

This list is by no means all-inclusive or exhaustive. Begin by circling those here that apply to you or any ancestor you know of, and then ask the Lord to reveal any others.

Use the prayer list that follows, and pray points one through seven of the prayer directive for each group individually. Then pray points eight and nine.

1. **Addictions**
   Alcohol; food; any prescription drugs or street drugs; hoarding; emotional or physical abuse; sexual sins; smoking; overworking; video games; television; internet; gambling; profanity; pornography; internet games

2. **Control**
   Possessiveness; manipulation; rebellion; unbelief; tardiness; uncleanness; criticalness; intimidation; co-dependency; stubbornness; domination; broken promises

3. **Death**
   Disappointment; murder; miscarriages; untimely or traumatic death; abortion; stillbirth; unresolved grief or loss; war death; suicide

4. **Family/Culture**
   Hereditary diseases; broken marriage; divorce; unhealthy ties with biological and extended family; rebelliousness; father not teaching children the ways of God; abandonment; parental

inversion; unworthiness; low self-esteem; unlawful actions; illegitimate son or daughter; family secrets; lack of communication; not feel safe or loved

5. **Guilt and Fears**

   Death; destruction; hatred; bitterness; false guilt; shame; fears of all kinds

6. **Injustice**

   Unfairly punished; favored siblings; blame spouse or self; lack of intimacy and communication; men dominant over women or opposite; sibling rivalry; rights; feuds; silent treatment

7. **Mental Illness**

   Anxiety; depression; bipolar disorder; ADD or ADHD; schizophrenia; phobias; oversleeping; withdrawal; isolation

8. **Money Extremes**

   Greed; poverty; status seeking; job robbery; devourer; over spending; stealing; business financial losses; deceptive business practices; bankruptcy

9. **Negative Emotions**

   Anger; bitterness; rage; violence; domination; fear; pride; resentment; hatred of men or women; emotional dependence; prejudice; revenge; jealousy; envy; unforgiveness; lack of intimacy

10. **Physical Infirmities**

    Sickly; weak; unable to work; infirmities; sleep apnea; asthma; high blood pressure; heart disease; cancer; diabetes; diseases of any kind

11. **Rejection**

    Divorce; separation; adoption; death; abuse; over protection; isolation; perfectionism; rage; violence; insecurity; martyr/victim; self-pity; hopelessness; shame; betrayal; unfulfilled destiny

12. **Religious Restrictions/Oppression**

    Domination; control; other religions; cults (Mormons, Freemasonry, etc.); occult involvement (be specific); supernatural powers; psychic powers; idolatry; witchcraft; satanic ritual abuse

13. **Sexual Sins**

    Fornication; adultery; perversions; pornography; masturbation; abuse; rape; being illegitimate; molestation; incest; fantasy

14. **Other**

    Pride; arrogance; lying; etc.

Note

Remember to keep all of your completed lists in the workbook until you have walked through the entire process. You may need to refer back to them occasionally. It is also recommended that you keep a separate list (below) to document all the lies about yourself that will be uncovered as you go through the *inner healing* process. We will be covering *ungodly beliefs* in chapter 7. However, if you recognize any lies before you arrive at that chapter, write them down below.

After thinking about each of the ones circled above, make a list of judgments or possible judgments you may have made. You do not have to have feelings or emotions; it may be just logical that you have probably judged them.

I Judged My Father; Mother; Leaders; Bosses; Authorities in My Life

Use this work sheet or a separate piece of paper to make your list.

<u>1</u>

<u>2</u>

<u>3</u>

<u>4</u>

<u>5</u>

<u>6</u>

<u>7</u>

As mentioned earlier, it is always best to go through these steps of *inner healing* with someone you trust; someone you know, who will not judge you, as well as being able to exhort you, and show you Christ's love and comfort.

(4) Restoring the Foundations–Family Patterns–page 397 by Rev. Chester and Betsey Kylstra

Prayer for Bitterroot Judgment/Expectancy

Now pray for each one separately:

1. Father, I forgive _____ for hurting me by _____.
2. I forgive _____ and release them from all punishment they are due.
3. I bless _____ with your love and acceptance. Lord reveal yourself to them as the God of love.
4. Father, forgive me for judging _____. I confess my sin for judging and ask for your forgiveness and cleansing in accordance to **1 John 1:9**.
5. Father, I accept the work you did on the cross for me. You became sin so I could become righteous. I apply the power of the cross to the judgment I made concerning _____.
6. (Firmly declare) I renounce and break any and all *agreements* I made with all powers of darkness for me and all of my descendants.
7. Satan and all demons that came to attack me and my descendants through this judgment, get out of my life Now!
8. Lord, reverse the old pattern and habit of judging and holding bitterness and my resulting reaction; please help its exact opposite to happen! Restore me to new life!
9. Father, fill me with the Holy Spirit and your river of love.

Did you feel a release in your body, soul or spirit as you prayed the above prayer? If yes, go to the following "maintenance" section below. If not, it could be that there is a deeper root of bitterness.

We have seen that bitterness has three stages. One is surface: something very bad happens and we became bitter towards that person. If we can catch it soon after the event took place, we can often easily forgive the person and repent of the bitterness towards them.

If we don't catch it quickly, the bitterness gets into our mind and becomes somewhat obsessive. With repeated prayers of forgiveness and release, however, it gradually leaves.

Lastly, is what we call *"bitterness of spirit."* The bitterness becomes completely obsessive. Our minds are consumed by the circumstances to the point where it robs us of all joy and peace in our lives. Having suffered through this myself, I fortunately found an answer that worked in getting rid of the bitterness in my heart.

We obviously have to forgive the person for the wrong done and genuinely repent for hanging onto the sin of bitterness towards them. Then every time we think of it, we must make a conscious decision to *let it go* (**Eph. 4:31-32**). For me, I had to do this dozens of times a day for weeks. As a result of my persistence to rid myself of the bitterness in my life, gradually I needed only to let it go a few times a day until it finally left. It no longer had control of my mind. The secret to this success is to persevere, even if you have to do it a thousand times. You don't need to keep forgiving the person over and over that you have bitterness towards. The idea is to pray that God would help you let it go and eventually it will be completely gone from your mind. It will no longer have control over you. The breakthrough is often a process but when you finally come to the realization that you have indeed been set free, we say WOW! Thank You Jesus! Please help me keep from bitterness, always.

Maintenance–Bitterroot Judgment/Expectancy

Continue in prayer for the Lord to reveal judgments and expectations to you. This is an ongoing discipline. It will seem overwhelming for a while but eventually you will make headway. I ask for a blanket of mercy to suppress the judgments while they are being revealed. Bring death to habitual practices of thoughts, feelings, and actions. Bring to life the Christ nature in you!

The following are some concepts we need to follow in order to be released from bitterroot judgment/expectancy.

Prayers of Forgiveness

Prayers like "I forgive you, dad for..." or "Lord, I forgive my mom for..." Then follow with "Lord, forgive me for judging/resenting/hating my dad or mom. Forgive me for perpetuating those attitudes in my present relationships." These are only conversations with the Lord not parents!

I guarantee the Lord will forgive you. He said so!

1 John 1:9

> *If we acknowledge our sins, then since he is trustworthy and just, he will forgive them and purify us from all wrong-doing.* (CJV)

If we don't forgive ourselves (as well as others), we can hold our own sins to us and keep us in spiritual bondage. When we don't forgive ourselves, it also implies that we are bigger than God because the bible promises that if we ask the Lord for forgiveness, He will cast those sins as far as the east is from the west.

If we don't forgive ourselves therefore, we are putting ourselves above God. This is a BIG don't.

Self-Denial

Luke 9:23-24

> **23***Then to everyone he said: "If anyone wants to come after me, let him say 'No' to himself, take up his execution-stake daily and keep following me.* **24***For whoever tries to save his own life will destroy it, but whoever destroys his life on my account will save it.' (CJV)*

We tear out those poisoned roots of our trees and cut off the life to those poisoned branches (habits, attitudes, reactions, and actions), by taking them to the cross.

John 20:23

> *If you forgive someone's sins, their sins are forgiven, if you hold them, they are held. (CJV)*

Chapter 5

SINS TOWARDS OTHERS/SHAME

Definition

Any thought or action against another or myself that separates me from God and makes me feel ashamed; feeling ashamed when humiliated by someone's anger or actions in front of others. Things we have done to others that did not nor would have glorified the Name of Jesus. Sometimes the person doesn't even know we have sinned against them, but it is a sin nevertheless. Examples of this could be lust; jealousy, theft...

Scriptural Basis

1 John 1:8-10, 2:1-2

> **8***If we claim to be without sin, we deceive ourselves and the truth is not in us.* **9***If we confess our sins, he is faithful and just and will forgive us our sins and purify us from all unrighteousness.* **10***If we claim we have not sinned, we make him out to be a liar and his word has no place in our lives.*
>
> **2:1***My dear children, I write this to you so that you will not sin. But if anybody does sin, we have one who speaks to the Father in our defense–Jesus Christ, the Righteous One.* **2***He is the atoning sacrifice for our sins, and not only for ours but also for the sins of the whole world.*

Gal. 5:19-21

> **19***The acts of the sinful nature are obvious; sexual immorality, impurity and debauchery;* **20***idolatry and witchcraft; hatred, discord, jealousy, fits of rage, selfish ambition, dissentions, factions* **21***and envy; drunkenness, orgies, and the like. I warn you, as I did before, that those who live like this will not inherit the kingdom of God.*

Eph. 4:22, 25, 28, 31

> *22 You were taught, with regard to your former way of life, to put off your old self, which is being corrupted by its deceitful desires;*
> *25 Therefore each of you must put off falsehood and speak truthfully to his neighbor, for we are all members of one body.*
> *28 He who has been stealing must steal no longer, but must work, doing something useful with his own hands, that he may have something to share with those in need. 31 Get rid of all bitterness, rage and anger, brawling and slander, along with every form of malice.*

We have observed that after anyone goes through the processes of dealing with generational sin, bitterroot judgments/expectations and soul/spirit hurts, they usually remember many things that they have done wrong to other people.

Most of These Are Either the Direct Results of:
- o   Generational sin pressuring us to do something hurtful sin to someone.
- o   The consequences of the hurts done to us.
- o   We just believe that we are bad and hurt others before they hurt us.
- o   We are so afraid of being hurt again that we reject others to keep them away in order not to be hurt again.

Regardless of the cause, it amounts to sins that we remember and, often, very much regret. Therefore, in order to clear our conscience, we must confess our sins to God, turn away from the sin, and put our faith in God who loves us so much. He is standing by, waiting to help us get a clear conscience. In order to facilitate this, we recommend that you make a list of all the sins you remember doing.

Many of us were taught when we came to Christ, that all we had to do was to confess that we were sinners and our conscience would be totally cleansed by God. NOT!

Testimony

A few years ago, I spent two hours a day for six months in the word and in prayer. However, after many struggles with my thoughts; rebuking the devil for reminding me of my past sins, I told God that His word didn't work. I was so upset. What came to my mind was, "You haven't done what the word said to do". I responded, "Where Lord?" **1 John 1:19** came to me.

After studying the scripture, I finally realized its real meaning. It says *"If we confess our sins"*- plural and specific. This is much different than what we are committing to at salvation.

After this, I spent months allowing God to search me and show me my wicked ways while confessing and repenting of the sins from my past. Great liberty came to me as I walked through this process in my life. Now that we know what to do, it does not take months, instead only a few days or hours before the Lord, to make such a list.

Do this by asking the Lord, "Please help me Lord. Remind me of all my sins that I have committed for which I have not confessed or repented from doing." It is important to include all things that you did for which *you are really ashamed.*

We may be tempted to not open up to another person to share these intimate sins, but hiding things in the darkness is the enemy's main way of keeping us in bondage. If we do the shame part of the list with a person who will not judge or condemn us and can still accept and love us,

it helps us to forgive ourselves and to believe that *God Himself can forgive us.*

Please do not leave out this step in your inner healing process.

To find all our sins may seem like an impossible task. Jesus wants us free–so just sit with Him. He was with you from the moment of conception and can help you remember the ones that opened you up to bondage from the enemy.

We *all* find it difficult to share our sins with another person. But share the sins; not all the details.

It is tempting to omit some of the more shameful sins because most of us fear that the person walking us through the inner healing process will reject us or think less of us, especially when specifically admitting the wrongs you have done. This will help them and us to remember how human we are

It's in the darkness and hiding that the enemy RULES!

The whole idea behind admitting our sins to God and to another trusted individual is to bring light into our lives where only darkness existed. Unconfessed sin from our past is like carrying a load of bricks on your back. When you expose the darkness, you are opening the door to God's light in your life and He takes those bricks and throws them as far as the east is from the west. You'll never have to carry those bricks again.

The reason it is so important to share the sins from your past with another person you can trust, is because when that person responds with love and acceptance towards you, as opposed to ridicule and judgment, it is easier to believe God can forgive you. Then we can forgive ourselves. Forgiving ourselves is also part of the process.

The Bible also says that it is the *truth* that will set us free. Confessing the truth about yourself sends the devil into retreat mode because he cannot live where there is light.

Prayer of Repentance

Make a list of the sins you have committed. One sentence for each is sufficient. The time I _____.

1. Now pray each of the following prayers for each item on your list. One at a time.
2. Pick a specific sin and try to remember the setting: where you were, and what was happening.
3. Try to visualize the event so you can play it over in your mind. Decide to confess and repent.
4. Father, forgive me for the sin of _____. I turn from it and return to you. I put my faith in you. Please cleanse me from its effects.
5. (Firmly declare) I *renounce* the sin of _____. I break the power of it from my life and the lives of my descendants, through the redemptive work of Christ on the cross.

6. (Firmly declare) I *renounce* and *break any agreement* with demons or powers of darkness over this sin. I cancel *all* demonic agreement and put the cross of Jesus between myself and any demonic caused by this sin.
7. On the basis of your forgiveness, I forgive myself and receive your cleansing in my life.
8. Satan and all demons that came through this sin, *get out of my life NOW!*
9. Father, take the grief and sorrow that came from this sin. I give it all to you now. (Wait as He starts taking it away)
10. Father, fill me with the Holy Spirit, fill all the emptied areas with your presence. FILL me now. **(Keep asking God to fill you until you get a release in your spirit)**

Chapter 6

VOWS, INNER VOWS AND SOUL TIES

Definition

A *vow* is a promise to perform a specified act or behave in a certain manner. A good example of this is a solemn promise to live and act in accordance with the rules of a religious order, such as the vows of a nun. A vow such as this usually implies such commitments as assurance, guarantee, oath, pledge, promise, undertaking or word of honor. A vow is a solemn promise or assertion, specifically one by which a person is bound to an act, service, or condition. A scriptural definition would be a promise or an obligation to God. Vows are usually verbally given in the presence of others.

Inner Vows

These are determinations of the soul–a decision made in our innermost being so that it becomes set in place. Inner vows take control to such an extent that all our energy and actions work thereafter to shape us in our personality and our life choices to meet or comply with that vow. These type of inner vows result in spiritual and emotional bondage.

An *inner vow* is an unconscious determination to take control, in an area of our lives, away from God because of a need to protect ourselves from repeating a hurtful or fearful event. The gist of it is that we see a behavior we don't like in another, and generally (sometimes unconsciously), we judge/condemn them for it. Then we make a promise to ourselves such as, "I'll never be like that"; or "When I grow up, I'm going to be like xxx", the opposite of what we saw; or "I will never do xxx." The heart can make a vow that the lips never actually verbalize.

The majority of the vows we make, however, are ungodly efforts made by us to set up protective walls around certain areas in our lives. "I will not grow up!" "I will never trust a man again!" "I will never have children!" "I'll get her back for doing that to me!" "I'll never be like my father." When we do this, we are saying, "God, I will take care of this area of my life, thank you very much. I can't trust anyone but myself for this."

At that point, we open ourselves up to the enemy's devices and, believe you me, we are no match for him. With God no longer allowed to be in charge of that area, Satan will take every opportunity to cause trouble. Since we made a vow to do, serve, or think in a certain manner, we feel compelled to do it or we feel guilty of violating our own conscience.

Example of an Inner Vow

One time this person approached me and started to yell at me. This lasted for three hours. I was totally crushed. It took me three days to pull all the pieces together following the ordeal. I told myself I would forgive him because that's what we are instructed to do in the bible.

Unknowingly, I made myself an inner vow, promising myself that I would never let him hurt me again. Shortly after I had made that inner vow, all the freedom I had gained over the years from inner healing work I had done seemed to vanish. I began to experience emotional struggles and fears all over again.

This was my conversation with God:

When I asked God what was happening, this was His reply: "You took your life back from me." "I wouldn't do that!" I replied. His response was: "At the point you were going to protect yourself, you became god of your life and therefore I couldn't be." I said to Him, "Do you mean that I have to let anyone hurt me?" He replied: "Just come quickly to my arms for comfort."

I asked God to forgive me for taking control of my life. I repented and submitted my life to Him anew. I asked Him to break through the bondage that caused me to make this inner vow.

What Do the Scriptures Say About Vows, Specifically in the New Testament?

Matt. 5:33-37

33Again the Law of Moses says, 'You shall not break your vows to God but must fulfill them all.' 34But I say, don't make any vows! And even to say 'by heavens!' is a sacred vow to God, for the heavens are God's throne. 35And if you say 'By the earth!' it is a sacred vow, for the earth is his footstool. And don't swear 'By Jerusalem!' for Jerusalem is the capital of the great King. 36 Don't even swear 'By my head!' for you can't turn one hair white or black. 37Say just a simple 'Yes, I will' or 'No, I won't.' Your word is enough. To strengthen promise with a vow shows that something is wrong. (TLB)

James 5:12

But above all, my brethren, do not swear, either by heaven or by earth or with any other oath; but your yes is to be yes and your no, no. So that you may not fall under judgment. (NASU)

The reason why both Jesus and James say not to make vows is that most often they force us to act or think in a certain manner, which is inconsistent with God's word.

Many times in a very bad situation we say to God, 'if you get me out of this mess'. In by so doing, we are actually bargaining with God by promising to do or not to do something. This is an inner vow.

Deut. 23:21

> *If you make a vow to the LORD your God, do not be slow to pay it, for the LORD your God will certainly demand it of you and you will be guilty of sin.* (NIV)

Exception

An exception to this principle is the *marriage vow*. Marriage vows are really covenants between husband, wife and God. God is a covenant keeping God and loves covenants, but we must keep them for He hates covenant breaking.

Inner vows are usually made out of judgment/ fear and have an aspect of hate that makes them ungodly. Then bitterness and hate differentiates them from rational, logical decisions and honest assessments of situations. These almost always come out of some very negative circumstances/traumas that cause us to make an (inner) resolve that we will never allow that to happen to us again.

It is not so much *what happened to us*, rather more *what we think* happened to us or our friend or relative. We have reacted in a negative manner both mentally and emotionally and now made an inner promise to never let this kind of situation happen to us again. What we think is happening actually shapes our perceptions about everything in our future, similar events and people because of the inner vows.

Remember how Grant Mullen said *with each hurt or trauma the enemy places a Lie.* The inner vow is the process that the lie or misbelief takes inside us, to set us up for bondage. The inner vows are based on judgments and wrong appraisals of situations. (1)

Hearts of Stone (2)

A *heart of stone* is a malformation of character whereby the individual has an inability to receive love. It is resistant to change and can only be affected, that is softened and melted, by persistent prayer, touches of love, and the rebuilding of trust.

The heart is the seat of a person's mental and moral activity, both the rational and emotional elements of each. It is the *center* or *springboard* from which flows all *desires*, *motives*, and *moral choices.* It is the innermost part of man; it makes up our basic nature and comprises our basic motivation and is therefore what sets our direction and motivation.

After we make an inner vow to ourselves, we forget all about it. However, unknown to us, it is active in our subconscious mind, in our heart, and in our innermost being. Because of these wounds and vows or inner vows, we now have to protect ourselves so we don't get hurt like this again.

(1) Why Do I Feel So Down When My Faith Should Lift Me Up–Dr. Grant Mullen

We do this by turning our heart into a Heart of Stone.

Walls are built around the heart because of the inner vow. These walls become brick and mortar by which the heart is protected and made less vulnerable. The greater the amount of *defenses* a person has put up in life, the greater the amount of *hurt* is there.

This results in retreating behind our defenses and *isolates* us from human contact and intimacy. Many have wondered why they have so much difficulty being intimate with God or with others. The reason is usually because they have made inner vows.

Very Important NOTE

The very walls that we set up to protect ourselves also keep us from receiving from God or others, resulting in our inability to give of ourselves to God or to others. A *heart of stone* is completely contrary to the very thing the Bible is founded on... *LOVE.*

The Father loved us so much that He sent His Son to die that we may have fellowship with Him. Someone with a heart of stone would find it terribly difficult or even impossible to be in a loving relationship with God the Father or anyone else.

(2) Hearts of Stone Triple Encounter "Healing Hurts and Hearts" by Rev. Gerald and Marie Richards.

What Do the Scriptures Say About the Heart?
- o   Out of the heart proceed all evil thoughts and acts. (**Matt. 15:19**)
- o   All forgiveness must come from the heart. (**Matt. 18:35**)
- o   We become calloused of heart and can't find God in the process. (**Isa 6:9-10**)

God is *able* to open the heart to respond to the gospel message.

Bringing Healing to the Heart of Stone

Ez. 36:26-27

> **26***I will give you a new heart and put a new spirit in you; I will remove from you your heart of stone and give you a heart of flesh.* **27***And I will put My Spirit in you and move you to follow my decrees and be careful to keep my laws.*

Healing begins with recognition of each and every vow and inner vow and progresses through repentance. For each vow, inner vow and judgment, we need to ask three questions:
- o   What happened?
- o   What hurts as a result?
- o   Where do I go from here?

Principles of the Process of Healing a Heart of Stone

Hearts of stone are always to be dealt with in love. There *must be no condemnation or judging.* The unconditional love of Christ must be allowed to shine through. The person is locked in a self-made prison because of being vulnerable, possibly to avoid more ridicule or because of fractured trust at some point in the past. Their fortress must be penetrated and it will take time.

The problem with replacing a heart of stone with a heart of flesh is that a fleshly heart has feelings, both good and bad. It is vulnerable and can be hurt easily, but at the same time and in the positive, it is more receptive to feelings of joy and the presence of the Holy Spirit.

We must rebuild trust if one is to overcome a stony heart. Trust is something that is built over time with people who show that they are worthy of trust. There is only one Person in the universe that is totally infallible in His trust and that Person is Jesus Christ, who is at once both Son of God and Son of Man. [2]

Steps for Healing and Breaking Vows and Inner Vows

Sit with God and ask Him to help you make a list of all vows and inner vows. One way to accomplish this is to look at the list of hurts and ask God what inner vows did you make or could you have made from these hurts. If it doesn't come, you may need someone close to you to help you think this through and make a list with you.

(2) Healing Hurts and Hearts – Rev. Gerry and Marie Richards

List of Vows and Inner Vows

Use this worksheet or use a separate piece of paper so you can use this book with others.

1
2
3
4
5
6
7

Prayer for Vows and Inner Vows

For each vow or inner vow, pray the prayers below.

1. Father, forgive me for making the vow or inner vow that _____. I turn from it, return to you, and put my faith in you. Please cleanse me from its effect.
2. On the basis of your forgiveness Lord, I choose to forgive myself for involvement in these vows/ judgments.
3. Satan, I renounce you and all the control you have in me through _____ (specifically renounce any areas of control that you are aware of; i.e. fear, anger, hate, etc.)
4. Satan, I take back from you all the ground that you have in me through _____ all the thought patterns that came from this sin; (worthlessness, hopelessness, shame, guilt, etc.)
5. (Firmly declare) Satan, and all demons that came through this vow or inner vow, get out of my life NOW!
6. Father, take the grief, sorrow, and shame that came from this sin. I give it all to you now.
7. Father, fill me with the Holy Spirit, fill all the emptied areas with your presence. FILL me now. (Keep asking God to fill you until you get a release in your spirit. Peace, comfort and the sense of feeling lighter are all indicators that God is answering your prayers.)

Soul Ties

Definition

Soul ties are an ungodly covenant with another person, based on an unhealthy emotional or sexual relationship. *Soul ties are invisible ties that bind us to another person.* God "allows" or recognizes these covenants. He leaves us free to decide when and if we will appropriate His provision to break/cut these ties and release both ourselves and the person with whom we have a soul tie with.

In this part of the chapter, we will focus on ungodly soul ties that create emotional and spiritual connections with another person that are perverted, dysfunctional, sexual, co-dependent, or controlling.

Example

Imagine that you have a number of ropes attached to your waist. Imagine also that the ropes are connected to each person with whom you have had an unhealthy emotional relationship. Now imagine more ropes connecting you to each person with whom you have had a sexual relationship. These ropes exert a subtle pressure that pulls you toward each of these people. As you try to move forward in life, you feel pulled in many directions at the same time. If you are married and you try to make love to your spouse, you often have memories of other lovers at the same time. They can even make you feel you married the wrong person, since you think of them. *You don't feel free and you are not free. These soul ties need to be broken one at a time.*

One reason God doesn't condone sex before or outside of marriage is because He knows that any demonic activity from one person transfers to the other during the sexual act. (The two become one.) This is a hindrance and the enemy has constant access from all ancestral sins and curses. The result of this also causes all present sins and demonic activity in both individuals to transfer to each other until these soul ties are broken.

1 Cor. 6:15-16

> **15**Do you not know that your bodies are members of Christ Himself? Shall I then take the members of Christ and unite them with a prostitute? Never! **16**Do you not know that he who unites himself with a prostitute is one with her body? For it is said, "The two will become one flesh."

Soul ties are usually co-dependent relationships where both individuals trust each other for support in place of the Lord so they get disappointed. The result of this is normally disappointment and deep hurts.

Rom. 10:11

For the Scripture says, "Whoever believes in Him will not be disappointed."

Balance

Be aware that Godly soul ties also exist in healthy parent-child relationships, healthy marriages, and mature friendships. An example of a healthy soul tie in the bible is between David and Jonathan. These are good soul ties and God wants more of them—with those who are mentoring, or close prayer partners, for example. We certainly don't seek to break Godly soul ties. Our God is a merciful God, but His desire, whenever possible, is that we maintain the healthy covenants we make, such as the marriage vow.

<u>Questions to Ask to ascertain if a Relationship is Healthy or Unhealthy</u>
- o   Is each person free to be himself/herself and to move toward their purpose in life?
- o   Is the relationship inhibiting to them in any way?
- o   Is it negative?
- o   Is it built on unhealthy, conditional love?
- o   Is there a healthy balance of exhorting each other as opposed to focusing on the negative traits of the other? Remember that no one is perfect.

An example of a soul tie becoming a concern is where one spouse has not *emotionally* left their mother and father to cleave to their mate. This soul tie MUST be broken in order for the marriage to succeed.

Another common one is where there is a family business and the expectation is for the son or daughter to work at or even take over the family business. In this situation, the parents almost always seem to exercise an unhealthy control over the lives of the younger married couple.

Gen. 2:24

>   *For this reason a man will leave his father and mother, and be united to his wife, and they will become one flesh.*

COMMUNICATION BREAKDOWN IN MARRIAGE [3]

THE EFFECT OF DEFRAUDING IN DATING

Lascivious (Lust) He becomes interested By sexual attraction	They come together on a physical level and disregard need for spiritual oneness		Defrauding She attracts him by dress & actions
Wrong morals He wants to prove love Fears losing her	Both lower their standards They withdraw & want to be alone more		More concerned that he likes her Guilt suppressed
He feels love is sex Shows his love to get physical involvement	Each is unable to find the real self of each other. Arguments & Break-ups		Seeds of doubt & distrust come between them.
He views marriage as Good way to meet His physical needs	Speaks of his love only when they are intimate.	Develops coldness Communication Breakdown!	She questions her husbands love Only what he gets
He gets angry at her Coolness as needs Don't get met.	Becomes more argumentative & demanding	Withdraws, worries loses confidence or dominant	Inner guilt from not fulfilling his needs as wife
He realizes To regain her love Proves his love To her	Buys things Financial problems result.	Begins to substitute kids & things for Husbands love.	Accepts situation Feels God is pun- ishing her or wrong Mate.
Thoughts he married wrong one. Thinks of Unfaithfulness.	Goes his own way. Tries to be fulfilled at work.	She becomes deeply hurt, is Critical and Suspicious	She doesn't care anymore and Gives up!

(3) Institute in Basic Youth Conflict Rev. Bill Gothard

How to Break Soul Ties!

Make a list by sitting with the Lord, asking Him to bring to mind all the people with whom you have had unhealthy emotional control or sexual ties. If all you remember is a face, that's fine, continue the prayer for each one.

List of Soul Ties

<u>**1**</u>

<u>**2**</u>

<u>**3**</u>

<u>**4**</u>

<u>**5**</u>

<u>**6**</u>

<u>**7**</u>

Don't feel ashamed as you share these with the leader. They are there to help you understand that forgiveness is complete. *Justified*. Just as if it never happened. That's why I love Jesus!!

Prayer to Break Soul Ties [4]

Note: Pray one through eight for each person on your list, one at a time,

1. **Pray:** Father, in the Name of Jesus, I submit myself completely to you. I confess and repent of each of my emotional and sexual sins, as well as my ungodly soul ties with _____ that I have been involved with in an ungodly way. I ask You Lord, to forgive me for my sin that resulted in this ungodly soul tie.

2. I choose to forgive and release _____ for his/her participation in this ungodly soul tie.

3. Lord, I receive your forgiveness. Thank You for forgiving, and cleansing me.

4. I choose to forgive myself and no longer be angry at myself, hate myself, be shameful, harbor feelings of guilt, or punish myself.

5. **(firmly declare)** Lord, I break my ungodly soul ties with _____. I release myself from him/her and I release him/her from me. As I do this Lord, I pray that you would cause him/her to be all that you want him/her to be, and that you would cause me to be all that you want me to be. (Pray this through for each person on your list.)

6. Lord, please cleanse my mind from all memories of this ungodly union, so I am totally free to give myself to you and to my spouse.

7. I renounce and cancel all assignments of all evil spirits attempting to maintain these ungodly soul ties.

8. Lord, I thank you for restoring my soul to wholeness. Let me walk in holiness by your grace. In the Name of Jesus Christ, I pray. AMEN.

(4) Restoring the Foundations–General Prayer Ideas–page 326

Chapter 7

UNGODLY BELIEFS $^{(1)}$

Part One

Definition

Ungodly beliefs are all beliefs, decisions, attitudes, agreements, judgments, expectations, vows, and oaths that do not agree with God, His Word, His nature, or His character. *Godly beliefs* on the other hand, are beliefs, decisions, attitudes, agreements, judgments, expectations, vows, and oaths that line up with God, His Word, His nature, and His character.

<u>**Scripture Reference for Ungodly Beliefs**</u>

Heb. 3:12-15, 17-19, 4:3
> **12***See to it, brothers, that none of you has a sinful, unbelieving heart that turns away from the living God.* **13***But encourage one another daily, as long as it is called today so that none of you may be hardened by sin's deceitfulness...*
> **15***As it has been said: "Today, if you hear his voice, do not harden your hearts as you did in the rebellion."*
> **17***...was it not with those who sinned...***18***And to whom did God swear that they would never enter his rest if not to those who disobeyed?* **19***So we see that they were not able to enter, because of their unbelief...*
> **4:3***Now we who have believed enter that rest...*
> **9***...a Sabbath-rest for the people of God.*

Everyone, to some extent, lives their life out of wrong beliefs. We call these "*lies*" about ourselves, about others, and about God. *Why are they so dangerous?* Because they affect all of our perceptions, decisions, and actions. This is why God wants our minds renewed, to establish our new belief system.

In this chapter, we will learn to describe the difference between Godly and ungodly beliefs. We will show how they relate to the sins of the fathers and *resulting curses,* soul/spirit hurts and *demonic oppression* and why we must minister to all areas and not just one.

As we look at how and why ungodly beliefs are formed, you will learn how to identify the most common ones. We will also learn the ways they damage us and cause us to live in a way that is inconsistent with who we really are as a person. We will explore the methods to rid ourselves of ungodly beliefs and replace them with true, Godly beliefs. You will discover how to re-program your own mind to think of Godly beliefs rather than Ungodly beliefs.

This will include the steps to take to break the power that ungodly beliefs have over our minds, and to appropriate God's power through replacing them with Godly beliefs. The belief system we have inside us is what makes us think, act, and live the way we do.

(1) Restoring the Foundations–page 157

Unfortunately, the lion's share of our belief system is usually made up of ungodly beliefs. Most of our beliefs about our right to exist, our purpose in life, our values and the very source of our security, as well as what we believe about our relationships with other people and God are ungodly. The more the Holy Spirit sanctifies and cleanses us, the more we have Godly rather than ungodly.

The goal is to be like Jesus; having only godly beliefs.

As Paul wrote in **1 Cor. 2:16**
    ...But we have the mind of Christ.

Most ungodly beliefs we have, appear correct to us because they are based on the facts of our experience, and yet, they are absolutely false when compared to God's Word.

Examples of this are: "No one loves me", "I am all alone", "I am defective", and "God doesn't love me." It is easy for us to tell someone else that their belief is ungodly. However, we are seldom ever able to identify these ungodly beliefs within ourselves. The reason for this is because *most of our ungodly beliefs are blind spots to us.* Much like the blind spots in the rearview mirror of our vehicles.

> **It is important** to pray through *each* of the previous chapters because doing only one or two will not solve the problem. You may get discouraged, but you *must* persevere to experience the freedom God has promised you. Each chapter is interrelated and therefore each *must* be completed in sequence.

It is very important that each of us participates in all the teachings on Accelerated Sanctification counseling we have covered, because doing only one or two will not solve the problems and actually discourage you, they all fit together as a package. The ungodly beliefs are very much connected to the sins of the fathers. In fact, we can often know which ungodly belief will be present in people once we know the sins of their fathers. The same sins that have plagued families for generations cause deception, clouded minds, rationalization, and unbelief in the same areas of your life today.

The sins of the fathers are like the hub of the wheel and the ungodly beliefs are the spokes. *Many* of the negative beliefs that we have about ourselves, others, and God result from the hurtful ways in which we have been treated.

Soul/spirt hurts often cause us to believe that we are not loveable, that we are not valuable, or important, etc. Soul/spirit hurts and ungodly beliefs are tied together, like two hands that are placed together with the fingers intertwined and locked.

The hurts must be healed and we must renew our minds. Unless this happens, the hurts will cry out messages of denial to override the attempted process of renewing the mind. Hurts are like infected wounds and ungodly beliefs are like the infection with the pus oozing from it. Both need to be healed. (1)

Ungodly beliefs are also related to *demonic oppression* and often provide the legal permission for demons to stay. For these reasons, we have systematically followed the progression in the workbook. Before we do ungodly beliefs, we will take you through the teaching on ungodly beliefs.

Usually it is best to do deliverance after all six spiritual areas have been dealt with.

- Generational Sins
- Bitterroot Judgement
- Soul / Spirit Hurts
- Vows, Inner Vows and Soul Ties.

Ungodly Beliefs from Two Sources[2]
Experiences of Hurt and the Natural or Unredeemed Mind

Ungodly beliefs are usually formed as a result of childhood hurts, traumas, and negative experiences. These beliefs will become incorporated into the very core of the hurt. Areas like abandonment and rejection cannot usually be touched until the hurts that caused the pains are healed.

Repetition of hurts reinforces the ungodly beliefs and statements like "You're no good" or "You'll never amount to anything", cause deep lies to be planted in our foundation of belief. In addition, negative experiences occurring during our adult years can cause further ungodly beliefs. (1)

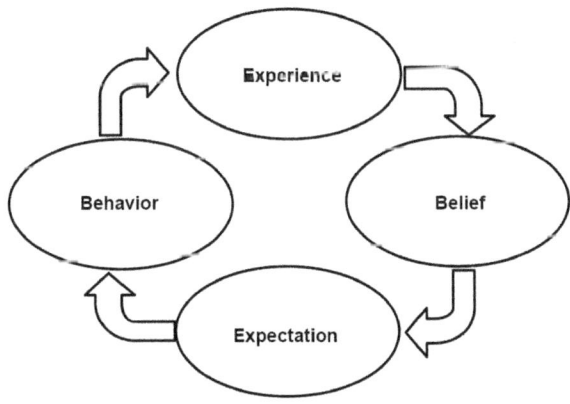

<u>BELIEF–EXPECTANCY CYCLE</u>

Pictured above is the *belief-expectation cycle* which is formed out of hurtful experiences.

As we start moving clockwise around the wheel, the ungodly beliefs become *expectations* arising from these ungodly beliefs. These expectations affect our *behavior*, causing us also to influence the behavior of others. This leads to *experiences* in line with these behaviors, which confirm the *belief* in the ungodly beliefs.

The cycle repeats itself and we build deeper, wrong and unhealthy foundations of ungodly beliefs. The only way to stop this cycle is to intervene between the experience and belief stages of this cycle.

We must choose to make God's truth our new belief. As we receive the truth and let it begin to change our beliefs, we begin to expect positive things in our lives. This leads to good behavior and good experiences. The new cycle of beliefs begins to be filled with truth and light in it, and this reinforces our new, healthier foundation. Now the law of sowing and reaping works in our favor rather than against us, as before.

(1) and (2) Restoring the Foundations Rev. Chester and Betsey Kylstra–pages 158, 159

A simpler example of this is when we sit on a chair. Our belief system allows us to trust that if we sit on the chair, it will support us. If we didn't believe the chair was capable of supporting us, we would not sit on the chair, for fear of falling over and hurting ourselves.

We have compiled a series of *common* Ungodly Beliefs about ourselves and for your convenience and reference what the Bible says about these lies in Appendix D.

Check each ungodly belief that you feel may be evident in your life from the charts below:

Appendix D

COMMON UNGODLY BELIEFS VS. BIBLICAL TRUTH ABOUT OURSELVES (3)

Ungodly Beliefs	Scriptural Truths About Ourselves (NKJV)	Additional Scriptural References
Rejection, Not Belonging		
I don't belong. I will always be on the outside.	**Rom. 8:15-17 15**For *you did not receive the spirit of bondage again to fear, but you received the Spirit of adoption by whom we cry out, "Abba, Father."* **16***The Spirit Himself bears witness with our spirit that we are children of God,* **17***and if children, then heirs—heirs of God and joint heirs with Christ.*	Eph. 1:3-6
My feelings don't count. No one cares what I feel.	**1 Peter 5:7** casting *all your care upon Him, for He cares for you.*	Prov. 14:29
No one will love me or care about me just for myself.	**Eph. 2:10** For *we are his workmanship, created in Christ Jesus for good works, which God prepared beforehand that we should walk in them.*	Heb. 13:5 Ps. 139:13-16
The best way to avoid more hurt and rejection is to isolate myself.	**Prov. 16:25** *There is a way that seems right to a man, but its end is the way of death.*	2Tim. 1:19
I will always be lonely.	**John 16:32-33** *Indeed the hour is coming yes, has now come that you will be scattered, each to his own and will leave Me alone. And yet I am not alone, because the Father is with Me.* **33***These things I have spoken to you, that in Me, you may have peace. In the world you will have tribulation; but be of good cheer, I have overcome the world.*	Deut. 31:6

Doing to Achieve Self-Worth, Value and Recognition		
I will never get credit for what I do.	**1 Cor. 3:11,14** *For no other foundation can anyone lay than that which is laid, which is Jesus Christ.* **14***If anyone's works which he has built on it endures, he will receive a reward.*	**1 Cor. 4:5** **John 9:31** **Matt 5:16**
My value is in what I do. I am valuable because I do good for others.	**Ps. 1:1-3** *Blessed is the man who walks not in the counsel of the ungodly, nor stands in the path of sinners, nor sits in the seat of the scornful;* **2***but his delight is in the law of the Lord, and in His law he meditates day and night.* **3***He shall be like a tree planted by the rivers of water, that brings forth its fruit in its season. Whose leaf also shall not wither; and whatever he does shall prosper.*	**Matt. 5:16**
Even though I do or give my best, it is not good enough. I can never measure up.	**Matt. 6:4** *That your charitable deed may be in secret; and your Father who sees in secret will Himself reward you openly.*	**Rom. 10:3** **Matt. 16:27**
God doesn't care if I have a secret life as long as I appear to be good.	**2 Cor. 7:1** *Therefore, having these promises, beloved, let us cleanse ourselves from all filthiness of the flesh and spirit, perfecting holiness in the fear of God.*	**Luke 6:43, 16:13-15** **Prov. 21:2** **1 Sam. 16:7** **Rev. 2:23** **Matt. 23:25-28**
I can avoid conflict that would risk losing the approval of others by being passive.	**Matt 7:24-25** *Therefore whoever hears these sayings of Mine, and does them, I will liken him to a wise man who built his house on the rock;* **25***and the rain descended, the floods came, and the winds blew and beat on that house; and it did not fall, for it was founded on the rock.*	**Phil. 3:7-9** **Rom. 8:28-29**
Control to Avoid Hurt		
I have to plan every day of my life. I can't relax.	**Isaiah 40:31** *But those who wait on the Lord shall renew their strength; they shall mount up with wings like eagles, they shall run and not be weary, they shall walk and not faint.*	**2 Cor. 1:20-22** **John 14:27** **2 Tim. 4:27**
The perfect life is one in which no conflict is allowed, and there is peace.	**John 14:27** *Peace I leave with you, My peace I give to you; not as the world gives do I give to you. Let not your heart be troubled, neither let it be afraid.*	**Ps. 43:1-6** **2 Tim. 1:7**
I must be in charge so no one can hurt me.	**Rom. 12:10** *Be kindly affectionate to one another with brotherly love, in honor giving preference to one another.*	**Phil. 3:7-9** **Ps. 23:4** **2 Tim. 2:7**

Physical		
I am unattractive. God has short-changed me.	**Rom. 9:20-24** *But indeed, o man, who are you to reply against God? Will the thing formed say to him who formed it, "Why have you made me like this?"* **21***Does not the potter have power over the clay, from the same lump to make one vessel for honor and another for dishonor?* **22***What if God, wanting to show His wrath and to make His power known, endured with much long-suffering the vessels of wrath prepared for destruction,* **23***and that He might make known the riches of His glory on the vessels of mercy, which He has prepared beforehand for glory,* **24***even us whom He called, not of the Jews only, but also of the Gentiles?*	**2 Cor. 5:17**
I am doomed to have certain physical disabilities.	**Prov. 18:14** *The spirit of a man will sustain him in sickness, but who can bear a broken spirit?*	**Prov. 17:22** **Prov. 15:13**
It is impossible to lose or gain weight. I am stuck. (idol)	**Phil. 4:13** *I can do all things through Christ who strengthens me.*	**Isaiah 41:29**
I am not competent/complete as a man/woman.	**2 Cor. 5:17** *Therefore, if anyone is in Christ, he is a new creation; old things have passed away, behold, all things have become new.*	**Col. 2:10**

Personal Traits		
I will always be_____ (angry, shy, jealous, insecure, fearful)	**1 Cor. 1:30** *But of Him you are in Christ Jesus, who became for us wisdom from God — and righteousness and sanctification and redemption.*	**Rom. 8:38-39** **2 Cor. 5:17**

Identity		
I should have been a boy/girl. Then my parents would have loved me more.	**Rom. 14:4** *Who are you to judge another's servant? To his own master he stands or falls. Indeed, he will be made to stand, for God is able to make him stand.*	**Rom. 9:20-24**
Men/women have it better.	**Gal. 3:28-29** **28***There is neither Jew nor Greek, there is neither slave nor free, there is neither male nor female; for you are all one in Christ Jesus.* **29***And if you are Christ's, then you are Abraham's seed, and heirs according to the promise.*	
I will never be known or appreciated for my real self.	**Eph. 2:10** *For we are His workmanship, created in Christ Jesus for good works, which God prepared beforehand that we should walk in them.*	**Philippians 4:8-9** **John 15:9**

I will never really change and be as God wants me to be.	**Psalm 139:13-16** 13*For You formed my inward parts; You covered me in my mother's womb.* 14*I will praise You, for I am fearfully and wonderfully made; marvelous are Your works, and that my soul knows very well.* 15*My frame was not hidden from You, when I was made in secret, and skillfully wrought in the lowest parts of the earth.* 16*Your eyes saw my substance, being yet unformed. And in Your book they all were written, the days fashioned for me, when as yet there were none of them.*	**2 Cor. 5:17**
Miscellaneous		
I have wasted a lot of time and energy, some of my best years.	**Rom. 8:28-29** 28*And we know that all things work together for good to those who love God, to those who are the called according to His purpose.* 29*For whom He foreknew, He also predestined to be conformed to the image of His Son.*	
Turmoil is normal for me.	**John 14:27** *Peace I leave with you, My peace I give to you; not as the world gives do I give to you. Let not your heart be troubled, neither let it be afraid.*	**Phil. 4:19**
I will always have financial problems.	**Psalm 1:3** *He shall be like a tree planted by the rivers of water that bring forth its fruit in its season, whose leaf shall not wither; and whatever he does shall prosper.*	**Phil. 4:19**
Safety/Protection		
I must be very guarded about what I say, since anything I say may be used against me.	**2 Corinthians 10:4-5** 4*For the weapons of our warfare are not carnal but mighty in God for pulling down strongholds,* 5*casting down arguments and every high thing that exalts itself against the knowledge of God, bringing every thought into captivity to the obedience of Christ.*	**2 Tim. 1:7** **Eph. 1:22-23**
I have to guard and hide my emotions and feelings. I cannot give anyone the satisfaction of knowing they have wounded or hurt me. I'll not be vulnerable, humiliated or shamed.	**Psalm 91:1, 5-7, 10, 11** 1*He who dwells in the shelter of the Most High will abide in the shadow of the Almighty.* 5*You will not be afraid of the terror by night, or of the arrow that flies by day;* 6*of the pestilence that stalks in darkness, or of the destruction that lays waste at noon.* 7*A thousand may fall at your side and ten thousand at your right hand; but it shall not approach you.* 10*No evil will befall you, nor will any plague come near your tent.* 11*For He will give His angels charge concerning you, to guard you in all your ways.* (NASB)	**Matt. 18:15-17** **Col. 3:12-15**

Retaliation		
The correct way to respond if someone offends me is to punish them by withdrawing and/or cutting them off.	**Rom. 12:19-21 19***Beloved, do not avenge yourselves, but rather give place to wrath; for it is written, "Vengeance is Mine, I will repay," says the Lord.* **20***Therefore, "If your enemy is hungry, feed him; if he is thirsty, give him a drink; for in so doing you will heap coals of fire on his head."* **21***Do not be overcome by evil, but overcome evil with good.*	**Matt. 18:15-17** **James 1:19-20**
I will make sure that (name) hurts as much as I do!	**Rom. 12:14** *Bless those who persecute you; bless and do not curse.*	**James 1:19-20** **Rom. 12:19-21**
Victim		
Authority figures will humiliate me and violate me.	**Heb. 13:7** *Remember those who rule over you.*	**Rom. 15:1**
Hopelessness/Helplessness		
I am out there all alone. If I get into trouble or need help, there is no one to rescue me.	**Rom. 15:13** *Now may the God of hope fill you with all joy and peace in believing, that you may abound in hope by the power of the Holy Spirit.*	**Rom. 8:28-29** **Ps. 23:4-6** **Deut. 31:6**
Defective in Relationships		
I will never be able to fully give or receive love.	**John 15:9** *As the Father loved Me, I also have loved you; abide in My love.*	**1 John 4:19**
If I let anyone get close to me, I may get my heart broken again.	**John 16:33** *These things I have spoken to you, that in Me you may have peace. In the world you will have tribulation; but be of good cheer, I have overcome the world.*	**1 John 4:16-19** **2 Tim. 1:7**
If I fail to please you, I won't receive your pleasure and acceptance of me, therefore I must strive even more. I must do whatever is necessary to try and please you.	**Romans 8:1-2 1***There is therefore now no condemnation for those who are in Christ Jesus.* **2***For the law of the Spirit of life in Christ Jesus has set you free from the law of sin and of death.* (NASB)	**Matt. 16:27** **John 3:16** **John 15:9**
God		
God loves other people more than He loves me.	**1 John 4:9-10 9***In this the love of God was manifested toward us, that God sent His only begotten Son into the world, that we might live through Him.* **10***In this is love, not that we loved God, but that He loved us and sent His Son to be the propitiation for our sins.*	**John 3:16** **Ps. 139:13-16**

They will just use and abuse me.	**Romans 8:28-29; 28***And we know that all things work together for good to those who love God, to those who are the called according to His purpose.* **29***For whom He foreknew, He also predestined to be conformed to the image of His Son.*	**Rom. 8:33-37** **Isa. 53:3-5** **2 Tim. 1:7** **Ps. 37:9**
My value is based totally on others' judgment about me.	**2 Cor. 2:14** *Now thanks be to God who always leads us in triumph in Christ, and through us diffuses the fragrance of His knowledge in every place.*	**1 Cor. 4:3** **Ps. 139:13-16**
I am completely under other people's authority. I have no will or choice of my own.	**Joshua 24:15** *And if it seems evil to you to serve the Lord, choose for yourselves this day whom you will serve, whether the gods which your fathers served that were on the other side of the River, or the gods of the Amorites, in whose land you dwell. But as for me and my house, we will serve the Lord.*	**Prov. 16:9**
I will not be known, understood, loved or appreciated for who I am by those who close to me.	**Phil. 2:13-15** **13***For it is God who works in you both to will and to do for His good pleasure.* **14***Do all things without complaining and disputing,* **15***that you may become blameless and harmless, children of God without fault in the midst of a crooked and perverse generation, among whom you shine as lights in the world.*	**1 John 3:1-2** **Matt. 5:16**
God only values me for what I do. My life is just a means to an end.	**2 Cor. 5:17** *Therefore, if anyone is in Christ, he is a new creation; old things have passed away; behold, all things have become new.*	**Ps. 139:13-16**
No matter how much I try, I'll never be able to do enough or do it well enough for God.	**Eph. 2:19-22** **19***Now, therefore, you are no longer strangers and foreigners, but fellow citizens with the saints and members of the household of God,* **20***having been built on the foundation of the apostles and prophets, Jesus Christ Himself being the chief cornerstone,* **21***in whom the whole building, being joined together, grows into a holy temple in the Lord,* **22***in whom you also are being built together for a dwelling place of God in the Spirit.*	**Matt. 16:27** **Phil. 4:13**
God is judging me when I relax. I have to stay busy about His work, or He'll abandon me.	**Col. 1:21-22** **21***And you, who once were alienated and enemies in your mind by wicked works, yet now He has reconciled* **22***in the body of His flesh through death, to present you holy, and blameless, and above reproach in His sight.*	**Heb. 4:9-11** **Rom. 8:1** **Deut. 31:6**
God has let me down before. He may do it again. I can't trust Him or feel secure.	**Isaiah 43:2** *When you pass through the waters, I will be with you; and through the rivers, they shall not overflow you. When you walk through the fire, you shall not be burned, nor shall the flame scorch you.*	**Ps. 23:4** **Deut. 31:6** **Rom. 8:38-39**

Consequences of Ungodly Beliefs

Our beliefs affect our identity, how we perceive ourselves, how we relate to others and the world around us, and most importantly, how we view God. They determine how Christ-like we become and even affect the quality of our Christian lives. Ungodly beliefs are live vise grips putting tight constraints on our lives and choking out the abundant life that Jesus promises. They are like spiritual termites that quietly work behind the scenes, undermining and eating away at the faith of God.

Ungodly beliefs are by definition, "unbelief". They hinder or block our faith in God and the truth of His promises. *When we live our lives based on them, we shut off God's ability to bless us.* (1)

Heb. 11:6

> *And without faith it is impossible to please God, because anyone who comes to him must first believe that he exists and that he rewards those who earnestly seek him.*

God doesn't reward unbelief or lack of faith. We use our ungodly beliefs to justify our fleshly behavior rather than allowing the Holy Spirit to sanctify us.

Rom. 6:6-7, 12

> *6For we know that our old self was crucified with him so that the body of sin might be done away with, that we should no longer be slaves to sin— 7because anyone who has died has been freed from sin. 12Therefore do not let sin reign in your mortal body so that you obey its evil desires.*

(3) Restoring the Foundations–pages 161-163)–Rev. Chester and Betsey Kylstra

Scriptures That Confirm the Hazards of Believing Lies or Ungodly Beliefs [4]

Rom. 1:18, 21, 24-25, 28, 32; 2:6, 8

> *18The wrath of God is being revealed from heaven against all the godlessness and wickedness of men who suppress the truth by their wickedness...21For although they knew God, they neither glorified him as God nor gave thanks to him...24Therefore God gave them over in the sinful desires of their hearts to sexual impurity for the degrading of their bodies with one another. 25They exchanged the truth of God for a lie...28Furthermore, since they did not think it worthwhile to retain the knowledge of God, he gave them over to a depraved mind...32Although they know God's righteous decree...they not only continue to do these very things but also approve of those who practice them...*
> *2:6God "will give to each person according to what he has done"...8But for those who are self-seeking and who reject the truth and follow evil, there will be wrath and anger*

2 Cor. 4:3-4

> **3***But if our gospel be hid, it is hid to them that are lost:* **4***In whom the god of this world hath blinded the minds of them which believe not, lest the light of the glorious gospel of Christ, who is the image of God, should shine unto them.* (KJV)

1 Tim. 4:1-3

> **1***The Spirit clearly says that in later times some will abandon the faith and follow deceiving spirits and things taught by demons.* **2***Such teachings come through hypocritical liars, whose consciences have been seared as with a hot iron.* **3***They forbid people to marry and order them to abstain from certain foods, which God created to be received with thanksgiving by those who believe and who know the truth.*

2 Thess. 2:10-12

> **10***...and in every sort of evil that deceives those who are perishing. They perish because they refused to love the truth and so be saved.* **11***For this reason God sends them a powerful delusion so that they will believe the lie* **12***and so that all will be condemned who have not believed the truth but have delighted in wickedness.*

(4) Restoring the Foundations Rev. Chester and Betsy Kylstra

Summary

Ungodly beliefs produce a *sinful heart of unbelief*, the mother of all sins. If we don't turn to the truth, we will exchange the truth of God for a lie, be blinded, seduced, and deceived.

Identifying ungodly beliefs in a believer's life is paramount if we are to enjoy all the promises appropriated to us through the shed blood of Jesus Christ at Calvary. It is our contention that ungodly beliefs hold the key to the liberation of many and in setting the captives free.

I encourage you to review this chapter on a regular basis. It is highly improbable that *all* ungodly beliefs will be identified during your first attempt. Continue to ask God for fresh revelations.

Chapter 8

UNGODLY BELIEFS (PART TWO) [1]

In This Section We Will Be Discovering: [1]

- o What they are, how they are formed, how they mess up our lives by being "blind spots", and what happens if we ignore them and don't do anything about them.
- o Truth has a higher level than the facts which our emotions remember.
- o How what we believe shapes our lives.
- o God's plan for our beliefs.
- o How to replace ungodly beliefs with Godly beliefs.

It's the Truth That Sets You Free–NOT the Facts

In order for us to be transformed into the image of God, our thinking has to be changed so that it lines up with *God's truth*, as opposed to the *so-called facts* that our memories recall (old tapes) from our bad experiences.

This is the Challenge!

First, there are the so-called facts that we remember. These facts are often distorted from what actually happened. The facts represent what we saw through our filter of ungodly beliefs and they are never the way God saw the circumstances.

The truth is how God saw it and what He says about it. God's truth is not seen by the natural man, who is looking at the facts as they remember them, but the spiritual man looks at the past through the faith of God and through His eyes.

1 Cor. 2:14-15

> **14** *The man without the Spirit does not accept the things that come from the Spirit of God, for they are foolishness to him, and he cannot understand them, because they are spiritually discerned.* **15** *The spiritual man makes judgment about all things, but he himself is not subject to any man's judgment*

We are spiritual people who are born again and are alive in Christ. Therefore, we are able to learn to see things God's way. We need to say "Lord, help me to be that spiritual person who can discern and embrace my experiences by the light of your truth."

Importance of What We Believe

Without faith it is impossible to please God. Faith in God and in His word opens the door of divine nature, divine character, and brings redemption of all of our hurts, wounds, rejections, ungodly beliefs, etc.

(1) Restoring the Foundations–page 175 Rev. Chester and Betsy Kylstra's

This principle is crucial if we are to experience the healing promised to us in the Bible, as well as to catapult us into a new and refreshing relationship with Jesus Christ as our Lord and Savior.

Acts 16:31

Believe on the Lord Jesus Christ, and you will be saved.

Rom. 10:9-10

9 *That if you confess with your mouth, "Jesus is Lord," and believe in your heart that God raised him from the dead, you will be saved.* **10** *For it is with your heart that you believe and are justified, and it is with your mouth that you confess and are saved.*

We must believe deep down in the central portion of ourselves. If we plant seeds contrary to God's word in our heart, we will sooner or later reap a harvest of like contrary nature.

The Following Scriptures Prove How Our Beliefs Can Shape Our Lives

Mark 11:22-24

22 *Then Jesus said to the disciples, "Have faith in God.* **23** *I assure you that you can say to this mountain, 'May God lift you up and throw you into the sea,' and your command will be obeyed. All that's required is that you really believe and do not doubt in your heart.* **24** *Listen to Me! You can pray for anything, and if you believe, you will have it.*

Prov. 23:7

For as he thinks in his heart, so is he. (NKJV)

Gal. 6:7-8

7 *Don't be misled. Remember that you can't ignore God and get away with it. You will always reap what you sow!* **8** *Those who live only to satisfy their own sinful desires will harvest the consequences of decay and death. But those who live to please the spirit will harvest everlasting life from the Spirit.* (NLT)

Matt 7:1-2

> *Stop judging others, and you will not be judged. For others will treat you as you treat them. ₂Whatever measure you use in judging others, it will be used to measure how you are judged.* (NLT)

We can renew our minds by using our emotions to analyze our belief system.

Belief Systems Chart[(2)]

Old: Satan's Lies	**New: God's Truth**
Your performance + others' opinion = My worth	What God says about you = My worth
Those who fail are unworthy of love and deserve to be blamed and condemned. (Fear of punishment; might punish others)	I am deeply loved by God Propitiation (1 John 4:9-10)
I must meet certain standards to feel good about myself. If I don't....(Fear of failure)	Justification (Rom. 3:19-25; 2 Cor.5:21) I am completely forgiven and fully pleasing to God.
I must be approved (accepted) by certain Others to feel good about myself. If I'm not approved...(Fear of rejection)	Reconciliation (Col. 1:19-22) I am totally accepted by God.
I am what I am; I cannot change; I am hopeless. (Shame)	Regeneration (2 Cor. 5:17) I am absolutely complete in Christ

(2) Search for Significance by Robert S.M. McGee page 231

Principles of God's Plan for Our Belief System
Renewing our mind is the first key.

Rom. 12:2

> *Don't copy the behavior and customs of this world, but let God transform you into a new person by changing the way you think. Then you will know what God wants you to do, and you will know how good and pleasing and perfect his will really is.* (NLT)

To know what is right and what God wants, we must renew our minds by reading throughout the scriptures. Once we read, pray, and meditate on God's word, we begin to realize that some of our thinking is wrong.

Eph. 4: 22-23

> *"Throw off your evil nature and your former way of life, which is rotten through and through, full of lust and deception.* **23***Instead, there must be a spiritual renewal of your thoughts and attitudes."* (NLT)

(2) Search for Significance–page 231–Robert S.M. McGee

Instead there MUST be a spiritual renewal of your thoughts and attitudes. There is an old saying that says *what goes in, must come out.* Instead of playing old tapes in our minds over and over all the time, we need to start inputting the *truth.* This can also be done by asking God to help us see ourselves through His eyes rather than our own eyes. *Prepare for a battle to get* new Godly *beliefs.*

The process of transforming our thinking must include *taking captive wrong thoughts.*

2 Cor. 10:3-5

> **3***For though we walk in the flesh, we do not war according to the flesh.* **4***For the weapons of our warfare are not carnal but mighty in God for pulling down strongholds,* **5***casting down arguments and every high thing that exalts itself against the knowledge of God, bringing every thought into captivity to the obedience of Christ.* (NKJV)

How to Identify Ungodly Beliefs

- o   Use the list of ungodly beliefs from the chart in the chapter
- o   Use the list of sins of the fathers; bitterroot judgments; soul/spirit hurts; vows/inner vows.
- o   Ask God to help you uncover other ungodly beliefs not on the lists mentioned above. Ask Him for fresh revelations.
- o   Ask God which ungodly belief is behind each issue you've listed. This usually digs up the root cause of our actions.
- o   Be aware of your actions. If there is an unhealthy response to a circumstance, ask God to reveal the ungodly belief.
- o   Ask a close friend or spouse to help you, particularly with the issues that upset you.

Voila! you have your list of ungodly beliefs!!

How to Replace Ungodly Beliefs with Godly Belief

There's an old saying: *the longest journey a believer will ever make is the eighteen inches from the mind to the heart.*

Writing down your godly belief (truth) is just as important as identifying your ungodly belief. The best way I have found, is to make yourself a worksheet with two columns on it. The left hand column will be to list your ungodly beliefs and the right hand column will be to match the ungodly belief with a godly belief, or the real truth about you.

You may find it hard, at first, to believe the truth about yourself, but I encourage you to persevere and you will eventually begin to see yourself through God's eyes as opposed to the filters of the past experiences in your life.

It only takes thirty days to break a bad habit. Repeat these godly beliefs (truths) about yourself for thirty days and you will begin to see a change in your belief system

I have great worth apart from my performance because Christ gave His life for me, and therefore imparted great value to me. I am deeply loved, fully pleasing, totally forgiven and accepted, and complete in Christ. Repeat this truth for one month...then as needed. [2]

(2)Search for Significance–Robert S. McGee

Take the necessary time to reduce the godly belief to one sentence and meditate on the corresponding scriptures from the list we have provided. This will not only ensure that what you have written down is a godly belief, but will serve to reinforce the truth about yourself.

All godly beliefs must agree with the character and nature of Jesus, as well as agree with the Spirit of the word. It is not always possible to find an exact match in scripture, so make sure the godly belief lines up with the positive concepts of truth in the Bible.

Write down all the ungodly beliefs about yourself which you have realized in going through this workbook and by seeking God. Then write down the truth and scripture provided in past chapters.

Ungodly Beliefs/Godly Beliefs Work List

Remember: every ungodly belief HAS an opposite...a godly belief.

Ungodly Belief (Lie)	Godly Belief (Truth)	Scripture
1		
2		
3		
4		
5		
6		
7		

Prayer for Ungodly Beliefs [1]

1. I confess the sin of believing the ungodly belief (lie) _____.
2. I forgive my ancestors who have passed down this lie to me. I forgive all others that have influenced me to believe this ungodly belief. _____ (names)
3. Lord, I repent and ask you to forgive me for living my life based on this *lie!!!*
4. (Firmly declare) I renounce the ungodly belief and break its power from my life. Satan, I *renounce* you and all the control you got in me through the ungodly belief _____! (Be specific. fear, rejection, hate, disappointment, not measuring up, anxiety, judging, unworthiness, jealousy, or shame)
5. Father, I give it to *you* now. Please bring your healing to my life.
6. (Firmly declare) I renounce and break all *agreements* my ancestors or I have made with the devil or with demons over the issues I've just mentioned.
7. (Firmly declare) I command Satan and all demons that came through this ungodly belief to get out of my life *now*! I cancel all agreement with the powers of darkness and put the cross of Jesus between me and any demonic activity due to this ungodly belief.

8. I now pronounce the *truth*, the godly belief _____ (opposite of ungodly belief.)

9. Copy down the truth and repeat it for thirty to sixty days. If you don't repeat the truth this whole process will not work. Transform your mind!!

After praying the above steps for all the items on the ungodly beliefs list, do the following:
- o Pray that God will bring an end to the effects of the ungodly beliefs.
- o Pray for the godly belief to be placed firmly in your heart.
- o That the word of God will be brought to the surface of your mind and be available for use as a weapon against future ungodly thoughts.
- o For the discipline needed for you to meditate on the godly belief every day for at least thirty days.
- o That the Holy Spirit will make you sensitive when you fall back into old thought patterns and will be able to take captive every contrary thought and that new thought patterns will be developed. [1]

<u>Things to Remember After This Process</u>
The *legal power of the ungodly belief is broken*, but you have to keep the doors shut:
- o **Take control of your thoughts**. Bring into captivity any that are wrong.
- o **Pray** to daily take responsibility to listen to the Holy Spirit as he shows you other **ungodly beliefs** and work through them in the same way.
- o **Fine tune** the godly beliefs so that they speak to your heart.
- o **Pray and meditate** on the new godly belief list for *at least one month*.

<h1 style="text-align:center">Chapter 9</h1>

SETTING THE CAPTIVES FREE

Definition

*S*etting the captives free or release from demonic oppression is commonly used to explain the pressure exerted by demons to get us to sin, to keep us bound in some sin; or to cause us to have wrong thinking. For years, many in the church have said demons are real, but that Christians can't have problems with demons. I believe most of us believe this to be false. Therefore, I will not devote much time to this issue. In the New Testament, the word for demon(s) appears sixty-three times. Jesus said in:

Matt. 12:28

"*But if I drive out demons by the Spirit of God, then the kingdom of God has come upon you.*"
This struggle is real and affects ALL of us.

Paul said of Christians in:

Eph. 6:12

For our struggle is not against flesh and blood, but against the rulers, against the authorities, against the powers of this dark world and against the spiritual forces of evil in the heavenly realms.

This Chapter Will Focus On:
- o   What are demons.
- o   How they get access to our lives.
- o   How to keep them from having access.
- o   How to evict them from others or ourselves.

What Are Demons and how do They Work?

The Bible gives no definite origin of demons. Most Christian leaders think that they are fallen angels, as described in **1 Peter 3:19** and **Jude 6**.

When Satan rebelled, he took one third of the angels with him as described in:

Rev. 12:7-9.

> *7 And there was war in heaven. Michael and his angels fought against the dragon, and the dragon and his angels fought back. 8 But he was not strong enough, and they lost their place in heaven. 9 The great dragon was hurled down— that ancient serpent called the devil, or Satan, who leads the whole world astray. He was hurled to the earth, and his angels with him.*

In the past, our society has said *seeing is believing*, and has discounted the demonic. But in recent years, there seems to be a return interest in the supernatural and people are turning to New Age and other occult philosophies. The increase in the number of psychic readers, tarot card readers; the reading of tea leaves, and performing séances, just to name a few, would suggest that people are more open to the reality of the supernatural.

Demons are invisible spiritual entities with minds, emotions and wills of their own. They are under the control of Satan. They are out to do his bidding and to torment the people of God.

We have often heard all the arguments about whether a Christian can be possessed. This argument stems from a wrong translation of the Bible. People have translated it as *possessed*, when it should be translated as *oppressed* by a demon, or *demonized*.

Tuck the following truth in your heart:

Possession implies ownership and no demon can own a Christian unless they give the demons complete control (often in the third world), but much more commonly, demons can harass them and make life miserable for them.

Their goal is to hurt God by hurting His children.

Demons are like hi-fi amplifiers that take a weak signal and make it stronger. They take our weak places of emotion, pain, hurt, fear, bad experiences, sinfulness, and bondage and make it much bigger than it really is. They amplify short-comings in our lives so they appear huge and out of proportion. They, to coin a phrase, "make mountains out of mole-hills". [1]

They try to kill, steal, and destroy anything that is good in Christians.

Some of us were taught that demons deceive us by mixing truth with lies.

This thinking is false, for scripture says in:

John 8:44

> *He was a murderer from the beginning, and abode not in the truth, because there is no truth in him. When he speaketh a lie, he speaketh of his own: for he is a liar and the father of it.* (KJV)

Demons try to keep people from being saved, and if that fails, they work to keep us from maturing and growing in Christ. They try to shut us down and make us ineffective. *Their chief strategy is to try to get people to turn away from God.* They do this through many forms of temptation and harassment, by trying to convince us that God is not good and His word is not true. Demons can affect our whole being. I do not believe that they can read our minds, but they are very intelligent and collect data on each of us. I believe they can predict what our responses will be to certain circumstances, since they have observed our previous patterns of behavior.

Demons Are Also Able to:

o   Make us physically sick.
o   Torment our minds with fear and lies.
o   Cause us to have painful emotions by condemning or reminding us of very painful words or events.
o   Weaken our wills by wearing us out— if we are not focusing on the truth.
o   Deceive us into believing that we are not loved and make us feel abandoned or rejected, even by God.

What Should We Do With Demons?

According to the word of God, we should remove all ground, handles, or doors that demons have in our lives.

John 14:31

> *I will not speak much more with you, for the ruler of the world is coming, and he has nothing in Me.* (NSAU)

By this, Jesus meant that there is nothing evil, sinful, or dark inside of Him. Therefore, the enemy had no access internally to Him. Commonly used terms such as *ground, holds,* and *doors,* are commonly referred to as access points that the enemy can grab a hold of in our lives (such as unforgiveness, bitterness, sins, judgments, vows, inner vows, soul ties, etc).

This access that we give the enemy allows him to torment us, deceive us, and rob us of our joy, and peace and a multitude of other blessings, which are our inheritance in Christ Jesus.

2 Cor. 7:1

> *Having therefore these promises, dearly beloved, let us cleanse ourselves from all filthiness of the flesh and spirit, perfecting holiness in the fear of God.* (KJV)

It should now be crystal clear as to what needs to be done and what our role is in it all. The following are excellent places to start, as described in the previous chapters of this workbook.

o   We must break all connections with the sins of our fathers.
o   We must examine our hearts regarding bitterroot judgments and expectancy.
o   We must forgive others (soul/spirit hurts).

- o   We must *confess and repent of all known sins* against o
- o   We must cleanse ourselves from all vows; inner vows, and soul ties.
- o   We must identify the lies of the enemy in our lives and replace them with God's truth for us (ungodly beliefs vs. godly beliefs).

Typically, after all this, deliverance and casting out demons is usually very easy. If we try to cast out demons *before* we have followed the order of inner healing as described above, it is then that we often find ourselves in a power struggle with demons since they still have legal right to stay in our lives.

If we try and go through inner healing and start by casting out demons, Christians will often quit out of fear that the demonic presence in their lives is bigger than God can handle, or more than they can handle. This is why dealing with the demonic is last in this workbook.

Satan is a legalist, and he uses the laws of God against us, unless we are wise enough to remove the *holds* and *doors*, thus removing any hold he may have on our lives.

When we have taken the necessary steps in the inner healing process, then we have the confidence to command him to go. With our authority in Jesus Christ, he *must* flee. He has no choice but to flee.

Who Has Authority Over Demons?

Every person who has received Jesus Christ as Lord and Savior of their lives has the same authority Jesus had in the bible, to cast out demons!

This is a truth! That means a new Christian has the same authority as a senior Pastor, once they know who they are in Christ Jesus.

Jesus told the twelve, the seventy, and all His disciples to *cast out demons*. He commands *us* to do it also...not to pray for it.

Just do it! It is your God given right, because you are a believer in Jesus Christ, the Son of God.

Luke 10:19

> *Behold, I give unto you power to tread on serpents and scorpions, and over all the power of the enemy; and nothing shall by any means hurt you.* (KJV)

Mark 16:17

> *And these signs shall follow them that believe; in my name shall they cast out devils; they shall speak with new tongues.* (KJV)

1 John 3:8

The purpose of Jesus' life was to destroy the works of the devil.

Acts 5:16

Peter prayed for people afflicted with demons and **ALL** of them were healed.

Acts 8:7

Philip cast out demons.

Acts 19:12

God did extraordinary miracles through Paul, *so that even handkerchiefs and aprons that had touched him were taken to the sick, and their illnesses were cured and the evil spirits left them.*

Many of our Christians have exorcised in the name of Jesus...numberless demoniacs throughout the whole world and in your city. When all other exorcists and specialists in incantations and drugs failed, they have healed them and still do heal, rendering the demons impotent and driving them out.

Three Methods to Drive out Demons

I have personally seen *three methods* of removing demons from people's lives. Sometimes, all are necessary, sometimes only one or two are enough.

1. Starving it Out

This is where the person receiving deliverance refuses to yield to the demon's temptations. Following a battle, the demon finds someone else more receptive, just like the story of the demons being cast out and going into a herd of pigs.

James 4:7 *...humble yourselves before God, submit to God and resist the devil and he will go."* (NLT)

2. Truthing it Out

This is where we memorize the word of God and every time the demon(s) tempts us, we use scripture to stand against it, by removing its ground by believing the truth that he whom the Son sets free is free indeed (**John 8:36**), **Matt. 4:1-11** (it is written), Jesus is quoting the word of God to stop the enemy's temptations.

3. Power Encounter

This is where we confront the demon(s) with the power of the Holy Spirit and force it out.

Luke 10:19

> *"I have given you authority to trample on snakes and scorpions and to overcome all the power of the enemy; nothing will harm you."*

How do Demons Enter?

The most common method demons get to have access to our lives are through our *holds* [SC: not properly described] or *open doors* as described earlier. They can't just come and randomly attack Christians, because we are under the authority of *Jesus Christ*.

We must do something to give them permission to harass us, with the exception of access through a sin or curse from one of our ancestors. The most common thing we do that gives them access is **SIN**. Every time the enemy lies to us and we *agree* with him, we are hooked.

James 1:14-15

> **14***But each one is tempted when, by his own evil desire, he is dragged away and enticed.* **15***Then, after desire has conceived, it gives birth to sin; and sin, when it is full-grown, gives birth to death.*

Gen. 4:7

> *And if you do not do well, sin is crouching at the door; and its desire is for you, but you must master it.* (NAS)

The wages of sin is death–*spiritual deafness*. Often we develop sin patterns and the progression of the following five steps is described as follows:

Ps. 19:12-13

> **12***Who can discern his errors? Forgive my hidden faults.* **13***Keep your servant also from willful sins; may they not rule over me. Then will I be blameless, innocent of the great transgression.*

- o   Error–one time
- o   To a secret fault
- o   To presumptuous sin
- o   To letting them not have dominion over me
- o   To the final great transgression–rebellion from God

The great transgression–rebellion.

Other places of entrance are *emotional or physical traumas.* These experiences fracture our defenses that normally keep demons out. He chooses this opportunity to place a lie in us during the trauma so that we can't separate the pain of the experience with the lie he puts in.

This is exactly how it happens with each of us. We eventually develop a stronghold for the enemy to live in us. If we do not get deliverance, he will slowly deceive us, and try to convince us to leave God.

Some of the Sins of the Flesh

Anger	Gluttony	Pride
Bitterness	Gossiping	Rebellion
Blaming	Greed	Self Righteousness
Covetousness	Jealousy/Envy	Strife
Criticism	Judging	Unforgiveness
Fear	Lust	

Another entry point is *passivity.* This is a state of mind, like being on drugs due to pain during surgery. Once again, the devil doesn't play by our rules; he has no morals and he looks for any opportunity to get into our lives.

Another entry point is when our wills are weakened during *illness or accidents*. Therefore, he often sneaks in when we are too weak to resist him. In times like these our defenses are lowered and the enemy takes advantage of us while we are down.

An obvious entrance for Satan is *occult involvement*. Many people have no idea that Satan is the author of all occult practices, because when we are involved in them, we are in rebellion to God. *What starts out as curiosity ends up as serious oppression!*

God hates the occult and there are many scriptures warning us to stay away, but many of us are totally ignorant of this danger. This doesn't matter to demons, as they will jump at every opportunity.

John and Paula Sandford teach in their videos there are **four levels of demonization**:

Infestation
o   Where the demons are not within the person, but gathered around them. It means that the demons gain temporary control in certain limited areas of our life because our sinful nature gives them access through unredeemed aspects of our character.

Inhabitation
o   The spirit has entered a person but has been corralled and is unable to affect much of the person's emotions and thoughts. The person's strength of character, aided by the Holy Spirit, has been able to resist the urging of the demon(s) and has shut it down.

Obsession
o   Where the demon(s) have come out of hiding to assume control of the person in certain areas. Here, the enemy has managed to install himself securely in some area of the person's character. In this way, the host person is obsessed and unable to maintain righteous intentions, such as an area of addiction.

Possession
o   *This is rare outside of the third world.* This is where the person has given total control of their lives over to the demon(s). An example would be serial killers.

Indicators of Demonic Activity
- One of the first indicators is when we realize that we instantly change moods. Not gradually, but suddenly and we are in an entirely different, negative place.
o   Incapacity for normal living, like the inability to feel joy.
o   Agitation in gospel or church meetings.
o   Often going from one extreme to another, emotionally.
o   The total inability to stop a sin or what we call extreme bondage is another indicator. Since demons masquerade as part of our personality, we often think that our unusual personality traits are normal. This can be demonic deception.
o   Exaggerated, intense, and out of control emotions.
o   A history of broken marriages.
o   Tragic accidents and accident proneness are often caused by demons.
o   Inability to pay bills when it is obvious that we should have enough money is a potential indicator.

- o Inner anguish. Especially when there is no particular reason. Like turmoil, depression, despair, mental lapses, and the inability to concentrate.
- o If we are unable to slow ourselves down, so we can't sleep, like a running mind.
- o Demanding too much sex, or wanting too little. Having opposite sexual desires of your partner, could be an indicator.
- o Going into trances could be demonic.
- o Super human strength can be caused by demons.
- o Unnatural phenomena. Like doors closing, someone walking when no one is there, and hearing voices when no one is present, are clear indicators of demons.
- o Self-inflicted injuries. Like cutting oneself or scratching the arms; suicide attempts are all signs of demons.
- o Pains that suddenly move from one part of the body to another. Sickness at inopportune times, like church or ministry times, are signs.
- o Sometimes demons manifest with very strong, foul odors, which have no medical reasons.

All these are possible indicators of demons.

How Best to Prepare the Recipient for Deliverance

It is best that the recipient be saved and very serious about wanting deliverance. We need their hunger for cleansing and their cooperation.

Since demons grab on to strong*holds and handles,* it is very important that the recipient has forgiven all who have hurt them, and repented for all current and past sins. If they have occult books, they should be burned. The receiver must know that Jesus has defeated the devil and all demons.

After all this is done, it is best but not always necessary, if sins of the fathers; bitterroot judgments; vows/inner vows; soul ties and ungodly beliefs are dealt with before deliverance. Then there is only one other area. That is to have set their will to want freedom in Christ.

Preparing Yourself for Ministering to Demonically Oppressed Individuals

Prepare yourself by reading scripture to build your faith, especially passages that show the power and Lordship of Jesus Christ. Use the Scriptures in this chapter.

Confess all unconfessed sin in your life to God. Make sure that you have no *unforgiveness* toward anyone. Be at peace and be confident about how much the Lord wants to set the person free. Pray for the gift of discerning of spirits to be active in your life.

The following lists are *potential* areas of activity or involvement, which has resulted in an "open door" for the enemy to come and torment, harass, control, or fill you with lies. We don't realize how much we are spirit beings and how these things can affect us. Circle the ones you feel may pertain to you.

Our first impressions are usually the correct ones. If in doubt, circle it anyway. It won't hurt to pray about it just to make sure. Keep in mind that while all these do not affect everyone, some people may be strongly effected by a few. In the west we don't realize how these can hurt us.

Activities and Involvement

Have you ever:

Cast a spell/Hex

Drunk blood or Urine

Owned Hard Rock music

Owned Heavy Metal music

Had Masonic Jewelry

Had Occult Jewelry

Had Occult Fetishes

Had Pagan Fetishes

Had Violent Rap Music

Heard a voice say "kill yourself"

Used Martial Arts

Made a blood pact

Played Dungeons & Dragons

Seen a satanic sacrifice

Seen demons

Seen Horror movies

Seen Evil sci/fi movies

Had a guru

Used mantras

Visited pagan temples

Visited Indian Burial grounds

Had your palm read

Used Yoga meditation

Seen a seance

Family Involvement

(Secret societies, cults, false religions, occult, and mind control organizations)
The following are examples of groups which omit the foundations of the Christian faith,
such as the Trinity, the atonement, the blood of Jesus, or the divinity of Jesus.

Altered Perception Reality
Armstrong/Radio Church
Anthro Physical Society
Astra
Baha'i
Black Muslim
Bubba Free John
Buddhism
Buffaloes
Catholic Spirit
Children of God
Christadelphians
Christian Science
Church Universal
College Fraternities
College Sororities
Confucianism
Cosmic Consciousness
Daughters of the Nile
DeMolay Lodge
Divine Light Mission
Druids Lodge
Eastern Star Lodge
Eckankar
Edgar Cayce
Elks Lodge
Esoteric Christianity

EST (Forum)
Father Divine game
Freemasonry
God Realization
Hare Krishna
Hinduism
Indian Occult Rituals
Inner Peace Movement
Islam
Jehovah Witnesses
Job's Daughters Lodge
Kabala
KKK
Knights of Columbus Lodge
Knights Templar
Masonic Lodge
Moonies
Moose Lodge
Mormonism
First Nations worship
New Age Movement
Nirvana
Odd Fellows Lodge
Orange Lodge
Rainbow Girls Lodge
Rebecca's Lodge

Rosacrucianism
Roy Masters
Santaria
Satanism
Satori
Scientology
Shamanism
Shintoism
Shriners
Silva Mind Control
Spiritualism
Swedenborgianism
Taoism
Theosophy
The Walk to find Self
The Way International
Transcendental Meditation
Unification Church
Unitarian Church
Unity
Voodoo
White Shrine
Wicca
Witchcraft
Yoga Meditations
Zen Buddhism

Open Doors for the Enemy

Infirmities/Disease	Fears	Sexual Sins
Accidents/falls,cars,trauma	Anxiety/Worry	Abortion
Arthritis	Be a burden	Adultery
Asthma/lung problems	Dread	Beastiality
Barrenness/Miscarriage	Harassment	Bisexual
Demonic Sex	Heaviness	Defilement/Uncleanness
Bone/Joint problems	Horror Movies	Evil Dancing
Cancer (all kinds)	Intimidation	Fornication
Diabetes	Mental Torment	Found Out
Fatigue	Paranoia/Phobias	Homosexuality
Female Infirmities	Superstition	Illegitimacy
Fibromyaljia	Stage Fright/Terror	Incest
Headaches/Migraines		Incubus/Succubus
Heart/Circulatory problems		Lesbianism
Psoriasis	Fear of being Abused	Lust/Fantasy Lust
Mental Illness	Fear of Authorities	Masturbation
Mind Binding	Fear of Abandonment	Pornography
MS	Fear of Being Attacked	Premarital Sex
Physical Abnormalities	Fear of Being a Victim	Prostitution/Harlotry
Celiac Disease	Fear of Being Wrong	Rape
Crones Disease	Fear of Cancer	Seduction/Provocative
Adopted Behavior	Fear of Darkness	Sexual Abuse
Appeasement	Fear of Death	Sex Play as a Child
Control	Fear of Demons	
Compulsive Lying	Fear of Exposure	
Denial/Enabling	Fear of Failure	Fear of Punishment
Domineering	Fear of Falling into Sin	Fear of Poverty
False Responsibility	Fear of Heart Attack	Fear of Speaking
Female Control	Fear of Inadequacy	Fear of Success
Intimidation	Fear of Incapability	
Jcalousy	Fear of Job Security	
Male Control Fear of Losing Control		
Manipulation Fear of Loss		
Passive/Aggression Fear of Man		
Possessive Fear of not knowing what to do		
Pride (I know best)		

<u>Occult Open Doors</u>

Abortion (Molech)
Accident Proneness
Animal spirits
Antichrist
Astral Projection
Astrology
Automatic Writing
Ball Gazing Crystals
Black Magic
Blood Pacts
Bloody Mary (game)
Books/Occult/Witchcraft
Crystal Ball
Death/Suicide
Demon Worship
Demon Dispatching
Divination
Dowsing
Eight Ball (game)
ESP
Evil Eye
False Occult gifts
Fortune Telling
Ghosts
Hexing
Hypnosis
Horoscopes
I Ching
Idolatry
Incantations
Light as a Feather (game)
Magic Charming
Martial Arts (some)
Materialization
Mediumship
Mental Suggestion
Mental Telepathy
Mesmerism Crystal
Necromancy
Non-Christian Exorcism
Numerology
Occult Movies

Occult Slavery
Occult Victim Omens
Ouija Board
Past Life Readings
Psychic Reading
Psychic Sight
Python /Leviathan
Reading Palm
Reincarnation
Religious Spirit
Sorcery/Omens
Spells
Spirit Guides
Stichomancy
Study of Demonic Activity
Superstition
Parapsychology
Table Tipping
Tea Leaf Reading
Tarot Card Reading
Telekinesis
Transcendental Meditation
Travel of the Soul
UFO Fixation
Vampires
Violent Dreams
Water Witching
Werewolf
White Witchcraft
Worship of Objects
Zodiac Signs/Charms

Other Open Doors for the Enemy

Violence	Trauma	Shame	Victim
Abortion	Emotional Abuse	Abandonment	Appeasement
Arguing	Physical Abuse	Anger	Betrayal
Bullying	Mental Abuse	Bad Girl/Boy (told)	Entrapped
Cruelty	Sexual Abuse	Condemnation	Helplessness
Death	Spiritual Abuse	Defilement	Mistrust
Destruction	Verbal Abuse	Disgrace	Pacification
Feuding	Accident	Different	Pacification
Hatred	Loss	Embarrassment	Self-Pity
Mocking	Imprisoned	Guilt/False Guilt	Suspicion
Murder	Rape	Inferiority	Low Self Worth
Rape	Torture	Illegitimacy	Unfaithfulness
Strife	Violence	Occult Involvement	
Torture	Court Case	Self-Accusation	
Mutilation	Self-Hatred		
	Insignificant		

Depression	Grief	Unworthiness	Failure
Discouragement	Agony/Torment	Inadequacy	Boom/Bust Cycle
Despondency	Anguish	Inferiority	Defeat
Gloominess	Constant Crying	Insecurity	Loss
Hopeless	Despair	Self-Accusation	Striving
Insomnia	Confusion	Self-Condemnation	Born to Fail
Loser	Heartbreak	Self-Punishment Loser	
Loneliness	Loss	Self-Rejection	
Misery	Pain		
Oversleeping	Sadness/Sorrow		
Suicidal Thoughts			

Mental Illness

ADD / ADHD
Alsheimers
Anxiety Disorder
Anorexia / Bulimia
Bipolar
Dysemthia
Dimentia
Obsessive / Compulsive Disorder
Schizophrenia

More Open Doors for the Enemy

UnBelief	Escape	Rebellion
Double Mindedness	Daydreaming	Anarchy
Doubt	Fantasy	Contempt
Lack of Direction	Forgetfulness	Deception
Mistrust	Hopelessness	Defiance
Mistrust of Authority	Isolation / Withdrawal	Denial
Rationalism	Passivity	Disobedience
Skepticism	Slumber / Oversleeping	Insubordination
Suspicion		Manipulation
Uncertainty		Resistance
		Self-Will
		Stubbornness
		Undermining

Addictions	Anger	Bitterness
Alcohol	Abandonment	Accusation
Cocaine/Crack	Frustration	Blaming
Crystal Meth	Hatred	Complaining
Downers/Uppers	Hostility	Condemnation
Heroin / Opium	Punishment	Criticalness
LSD	Repressed Anger	Gossip /Slander
Magic Mushrooms	Rage	Judging
Methadone	Resentment	Revenge
Non Prescription Drugs	Revenge	Hostility
Prescription Drugs	Temper Tantrums	Violence
Smoking	Unforgiveness	
Tranquilizers		

Motivation	Pride	Mocking
Drivenness	Arrogance / Controlling	Blaspheming
Irresponsibility	God-Playing	Laughing
Laziness	Envy/Jealousy	Profanity
Performance Oriented	Jezebel / Ahab	Ridicule
Procrastination	Fool / Haughty	Sarcasm
Undisciplined	Self-Righteous	Scorn
	Self-Centered	
	Self Conscious	
	Selfish Ambition	
	Self-Importance	
	Egotistical /Prejudice	
	Vanity / Exhibitionism	

Prayer for Deliverance from Sins and Demonic Oppression

Concept:

Remind the person of the great work Jesus Christ has done so that they can be free!! Read some of the truths:

Mark 16:17	Acts 10:38	Rom. 3:10-12
Rom. 3:23-25	Rom. 6:16 2	Cor. 7:1
Col. 2:15	Heb. 2:14-15	John 1:8-10
1 John 3:8	Rev. 12:11	

As far as GOD is concerned, He removed your sins as far as the east is from the west. He remembers NONE of your sins.

You are a new creation–the apple of His eye; all things are new for you. He has a great plan for you–Satan is defeated and Jesus is LORD!

Note Use lists on previous pages to make your lists. *Leader* will REBUKE the name of each group one at a time. The person says "amen" after each name, showing agreement with the process.

PRAY: Lord, I ask your protection for myself and my family and for those involved here and their families during this inner healing. We ask You Lord, to come and do what you do best, showing your power and might; giving us the revelation of Your Holy Spirit; the discerning of spirits to be active and your wisdom to know how to proceed.

PRAY: I give you permission to work in any way Lord that you think necessary. I ask you to reveal everything needed in order to get my complete freedom from demonic oppression. I also ask for the light of Your Holy Spirit to shine brightly on us and show us specific things that need to be revealed!

1. I repent and ask your forgiveness for agreeing and listening to demons and for catering to their demands and desires.
2. I forgive myself for yielding to demons for so long.

3. I forgive and ask forgiveness for the following sins and agreement with these demons, one by one. I take back all the ground I gave you in my life in Jesus name.

4. **(Firmly declare)** I renounce and break all agreement with demons and take back all the control I have given to you enemy, and put it all under the Lordship of Jesus Christ.

5. **(Firmly declare)** I command all demons working in the areas just mentioned to *leave* in Jesus' Name! I break all *agreement* with demons in my life and in the lives of my descendants over these issues.

   Now go back to the other groups and repeat this process, using steps three through five, until finished with all the pages. Then proceed to the steps below.

6. Lord, I ask you to reveal if there are any areas where demons are hiding or have failed to leave. Enlist the help of the prayer for any areas that the tension did not release. If there are, *re-do* steps three through five.

7. Lord Jesus, I command any demons who are still present to manifest... (If manifestations occur rebuke them in Jesus Name commanding them to leave).

8. Lord, please fill me with Your Holy Spirit, washing every area vacated by the enemy. (Wait on God until the cleansing and filling is finished, and His peace prevails).

9. Remind the one going through the inner healing that the demons will try to make a second stand, or deceive them into letting them back in. They *must* learn to *stand* in the *truth* that "whom the Son sets free, is free indeed!"

10. *Very Important*: Remind them to read through their Godly beliefs *every day* for thirty to sixty days and again if there is a need!) IF YOU DO NOT DO THIS, YOU HAVE NOT FINISHED THE PROCESS.

CONCLUSION

If you have read this workbook and training manual from start to finish and have completed the work prescribed in the various chapters, God bless you and may He reward you for all the effort it required. If on the other hand, you have simply read it to learn, we suggest that you go back and complete the workbook. We believe you will find it liberating and fulfilling. It is always better to do this with someone else that you trust. Once you finish, please help others.

We believe the end of time and the second coming of our Lord Jesus Christ is drawing nearer with every passing day and as such, we are seeing the beginning of the promise from **Joel 2:28** "*I will pour out My Spirit on all the people.*"

Many of the individuals who are coming to the Lord are coming because of difficult circumstances in their lives. They are coming with massive wounds and scars. We need mature saints to establish them as disciples of Jesus Christ with all the proper foundations of Christianity. It is our hope that this workbook and training manual will be used by you the reader, to help ground the new believers and even more mature ones who have never pursued accelerated sanctification.

Remember that inner healing is really an accelerated process of sanctification (ABCs) of the kingdom of God. Why spend years recovering from the circumstances of our past when it can all be accelerated so you can more adequately pursue the things of God for your life.

This is your day. If this has helped you, please send us a brief testimony to dan.d.chick@gmail.com. Go help someone else to be set free.

Remember, we are available to come to your church and teach all those interested

May our Heavenly Father bless you with all the spiritual gifts, favor and understanding which is your inheritance in the Lord.

BIBLIOGRAPHY

There are so many excellent books on this subject that we could not attempt to list them all. However, we want to give a short list of the ones that have been especially helpful to us, and were used in this book.

If you are serious about pursuing praying & counseling, these books will help you to be more effective.

1. <u>Restoring the Foundations</u> by Reverend Chester and Betsey Kylstra
   Proclaiming His Word Publications P.O. Box 2339
   Santa Rosa Beach, Florida 32459
   www.healinghouse.org/HHNrtfm.htm

2. <u>The Transformation of the Inner Man</u> by Reverend John and Paula Sandford
   Victory House Inc.
   Tulsa, OK
   www.elijahouse.org

3. <u>Institute in Basic Youth Conflict</u> by Reverend Bill Gothard
   www.iblp.org/iblp

4. <u>Triple Encounter "Healing Hurts & Hearts"</u> by Reverend Gerald and Marie Richards
   www.restorationministries.ca

5. <u>Search for Significance</u> by Reverend Robert S. McGee
   Rapha Publishing Houston, TX, 1990

6. <u>Why Do I Feel So Down When My Faith Should Lift Me Up</u> by Dr. Grant Mullen
   Sovereign World Ltd., Kent, ENG 1999
   Distributed by Renew Books, Ventura, CA
   www.drgrantmullen.com/aboutauth.html

7. <u>Forgiveness</u> by Reverend John and Carol Arnott
   Toronto Airport Christian Fellowship

Lightning Source UK Ltd.
Milton Keynes UK
UKHW050316060919
349269UK00002B/20/P